"Jay Milbrandt has his
and his generation is le
Do should be a playbook for anyone looking to answer God's
call to serve a hurting world."

—Rich Stearns, president of World Vision US and author of *The Hole in Our Gospel*

"Equal parts guts and grit, *Go and Do* reminds us that we all have an important role to play in transforming the world. You might be surprised what you will accomplish when you take your passions out for a lap around the world."

—Bob Goff, founder of Restore International and author of *Love Does*

"Jay Milbrandt captures the infectious energy rising from a generation that is facing our hurting world with faith and action. Whether it's on university campuses across America or in churches around the world, the "go and do" admonition captures our hearts and minds. *Go and Do* presents a question to each one of us: how might I serve to change the world, even if for only one person? This inspiring book is a call to action for every Christian."

—Judge Kenneth W. Starr, president of Baylor University

"*Go and Do* is a transformative read that will move people from knowledge to action consistent with the teachings of our Lord and Savior, Jesus Christ. As one who has traveled extensively and lived in many countries in the world, witnessing poverty, injustice, and suffering firsthand, I found that Jay Milbrandt's book *Go and Do* is both a highly recommended read and a call to action. I anticipate that the message of this book will lead to actions with eternal consequences. It is timely, especially considering the global crisis surrounding us!"

—Kadita "A. T." Tshibaka, president and CEO emeritus of Opportunity International US

go+do

go + do

DARING TO CHANGE THE WORLD
ONE STORY AT A TIME

JAY MILBRANDT

Tyndale House Publishers, Inc.
Carol Stream, Illinois

Visit Tyndale online at www.tyndale.com.

Visit the author at jaymilbrandt.com.

TYNDALE and Tyndale's quill logo are registered trademarks of Tyndale House Publishers, Inc.

Go and Do: Daring to Change the World One Story at a Time

Published in association with Yates & Yates (www.yates2.com).

Designed by Stephen Vosloo

Edited by Lisa Jackson

Scripture quotations are taken from the *Holy Bible*, New Living Translation, copyright © 1996, 2004, 2007 by Tyndale House Foundation. Used by permission of Tyndale House Publishers, Inc., Carol Stream, Illinois 60188. All rights reserved.

Library of Congress Cataloging-in-Publication Data

Milbrandt, Jay.
  Go and do : daring to change the world one story at a time / Jay Milbrandt.
    p. cm.
  ISBN 978-1-4143-6135-2 (sc)
1. Human rights—Religious aspects—Christianity. 2. Evangelistic work. 3. Change—Religious aspects—Christianity. 4. Change (Psychology)—Religious aspects—Christianity. 5. Milbrandt, Jay. I. Title.
  BT738.15.M55 2012
  248.4—dc23   2012003016

Printed in the United States of America

18   17   16   15   14   13   12
7   6   5   4   3   2   1

For Ami, Amey, Faifah, Four, Jupee, and Suwanan.
May I one day be able to return to you even
a fraction of what you've given me.

Contents

Author's Note *xi*

Prologue *xiii*

1. A Dare in the Desert *1*
2. In over My Head *11*
3. Losing Faifah *25*
4. It's Not about Changing the World *41*
5. Coming Alive *57*
6. We Are the Solution *67*
7. Bold Explorations *89*
8. The Great Tension *105*
9. The Power of Presence *115*
10. Use Words If Necessary *129*
11. Living Dangerously *139*
12. Making Goodness Fashionable *153*
13. All the World's a Stage *169*
14. Putting It All Together *179*

Epilogue *199*

Acknowledgments *205*

Notes *207*

Author's Note

Sometimes It Is about You

WE WERE RAISED TO BELIEVE that each of us is special. From day one, we're told that we're all unique, that we all have a purpose. We are promised that there's a college or job that is perfect for us. We can each follow our own course in life. We can live whatever we dream. Yet we often find ourselves at a crossroads where nothing seems to make sense anymore. That special, unique purpose doesn't appear to exist, like we got on the wrong train and we can't get back. You find yourself asking, *What am I doing here?*

What makes it worse is that we get mixed messages. If all these things we've been led to believe are true, how do we embrace a parallel message that life is not supposed to be about us? How can it be anything but about me when I'm still trying to figure myself out? And how do I respond when I'm told that I'm supposed to die to myself? I don't even understand what that means. I'm still struggling to live life for myself.

Sometimes it *is* about you. Sometimes you need to figure things out for yourself. If you've had that moment or period in life when you've asked, "What am I doing here?" then I've got a challenge for you. A challenge that might just change your life like it did mine.

Actually, it's more than a challenge; it's a dare. I dare you to make a personal revolution. I dare you to go out into the world, to witness the raw edges of life, and then to do something about what you see. I dare you to "go and do."

This book is my personal revolution. But it can be anyone's revolution. Because my crisis was exactly the same crisis that countless others are facing. I see it every day as I work with students who, like me, are asking, "What am I doing here?"

This personal revolution is not about changing the world; it's about changing yourself. This revolution will overthrow your inner constitution, but it will also rescue you. I needed to be rescued—and I was. But only because I was willing to step up to the dare I made to myself.

Those of us who have taken this challenge are exploring the deepest reaches of life and faith in order to find what makes us come alive. We are embarking on a journey that leads to discovering joy. If you want to join us, then keep reading. But I'll warn you, you'll imagine yourself in the pages and stories here. And if you do, if this is you, then you can't back down.

If you accept the dare, then you won't have it easy. To "go" requires taking a giant leap of faith—maybe the biggest, riskiest leap you've ever taken. And to "do" requires forgetting much of what you've been told. People will object—people close to you—and you may even try to talk yourself down from the ledge.

But if you stick with it, this challenge will change you and the way you look at the world.

Sometimes it *is* about you, and this book is about changing yourself. Welcome to the journey.

Prologue

WHAT AM I DOING HERE? I blink a few times and swipe away the mosquito netting as I roll off my mat and onto the reed floor.

Mae La Refugee Camp has just sprung to life here along the Thai-Burma border. The camp is bustling with activity. The roosters are crowing and the sun still has to rise over the mountains. I look at my watch. It's only 5 a.m., yet I feel like I'm the last one out of bed.

I stumble out of a makeshift bedroom enclosed by bedsheet walls and into another bamboo-hut-style room overlooking the camp. My hosts—residents of the camp—have already prepared hot water for me. I make a cup of coffee with a 3-in-1 instant mix. I rarely drink coffee, but this is perhaps one of the best cups I've ever tasted. Its rich aroma adds to the moment.

With the fog now rolling out of the valley, the day is beginning to warm up. It rained most of last night, so everything is still soaked—the sun hasn't come out enough to dry the area. It's peaceful. Quite possibly one of the most beautiful mornings I've ever witnessed.

Mae La Refugee Camp is essentially a self-contained village. It's nearly identical to a village in the jungle, except that it's brimming with tens of thousands of people who cannot leave. This "temporary" camp has been here for more than twenty years.

Last night I sat down with some of the youth to listen to stories of how they arrived here—how they became refugees. A boy in his early teens scurried up to me and began to relate his story as if I were the first person to ever express interest.

First came the mortar shells; violent, thundering explosions piercing the night and raining down on his sleepy village. The Burma Army was attacking. Everyone tried to run before the foot soldiers arrived, he said. Lines of soldiers marched into the village with the authorization to shoot on sight. He last saw his parents that night in the jungle—they all had to run, and in the commotion, they lost each other. Their homes were burned, friends killed, lives destroyed.

This young boy described how he had walked for seven days through a dense, dangerous jungle—mostly at night to avoid being killed or captured. Arriving at the border, he found his way to this camp, where he began a new life. Although the attack took place a few years ago, he vowed he would find his parents again. Until then, this small refugee camp would remain his home.

Before we finished our conversation, more of the youth gathered around to sing a song in their native Karen language (pronounced CAR-in). "Our Karen people are very tired and we don't see the hope," the song leader said. "But we hope that someday we will have our lives in our Karen State, and we will get freedom." Sitting cross-legged on the thatched reed floor before them, I wished I could do something to offer them freedom.

Yet, there's nothing I can do except show up and listen—just be with them. I've got no solutions to their plight. After the song, they ask a lot of questions about life outside the camp, especially world news. I can answer those. The only thing they ask from me is that I share their story with the outside world— they want to be remembered.

Is this really a refugee camp? I wonder. It's so beautiful and life seems so simple. Unfortunately, the people here can't leave this small island of a village surrounded by barbed wire and armed guards. They do not have the freedom they desperately seek. While the camp provides refuge from persecution in Burma, it's as much or more a prison than life outside the walls would be.

For me, ironically, the camp is an escape. I realize that I feel free. Here, I forget many of the things that occupy my mind in America. Life is less noisy and thoughts so much clearer. It's peculiar how one person's prison can be another person's freedom.

As I watch the sun rise, I try to think back to what brought me to Mae La Refugee Camp in the first place.

I had been trapped in my own prison of sorts—caged in by life's expectations and desires. I had wandered through my own desert until I finally gave in and responded to the cry of my heart for the world's deepest needs.

So, how did I get here?

A dare.

CHAPTER 1

A Dare in the Desert

WHAT AM I DOING HERE? My face buried deep in my hands, I was exasperated.

My head dropped into the textbook in front of me. As my nose lodged in the binding between two thick sets of pages, the aroma of ink formed the walls of my paper and knowledge penitentiary. My mind wandered everywhere except to the matters right in front of me.

What am I doing here? I whispered to myself in exasperation. The library felt eerily quiet this evening.

Why did I come to law school? I wondered. Everything had fit together so well—I was accepted at the school of my choice. I found what I studied to be interesting, and it seemed like I was right where I was supposed to be. But now, in the thick of it, I just wanted to be anywhere but here.

What was this all for? Would I graduate to work for a big law firm so that I could feel exactly the way I'm feeling now—for the rest of my life? Would I end up unhappy? It didn't seem worth it, no matter how much I might be paid or how big my house might be. Life felt too short, and today would be another day I'd never get back.

Maybe, I pondered, *I'm doing what I'm supposed to be doing, but I just can't see it yet.* It's hard to have perspective when you're in the thickest part of a dense fog. Still, it would certainly be easier and more fun to do something else. I started daydreaming about moving to Aruba to teach windsurfing lessons. I pictured the sun and warm water. I'd drive a Jeep around with the top down. I'd sit most of the day under a thatch-roofed hut, wearing board shorts and dark sunglasses.

I violently shook my head, bringing me back to reality. I detested my lack of focus. I stood up. I had to move around and stretch my stiffened body. A break might help me regain concentration. Walking to the window, I put my hands on the sill and leaned on it. The metal under my palms felt cold, giving a shot of life to my seemingly lifeless body. Gazing outside, I realized how everything looks so much more appealing when you feel trapped.

I didn't realize it yet, but I had wandered into a desert.

The first week of law school, I had attended church on Sunday morning. The theme of the sermon that day posited that throughout life, we find ourselves led in and out of deserts— periods of temptation and hardship. Although difficult, these deserts should be embraced, expected, and appreciated. I didn't like what I heard. The message felt uncomfortable—it felt like divine foreshadowing. A few weeks later, there I sat, in the desert.

Wandering into a desert is a little like getting lost in a car—you make a few turns that you think are correct and then all of a sudden you realize that you're lost and unable to backtrack. This realization almost always arrives in a single, rushing moment.

My moment of realization didn't hit until near the end of my first semester. All seemed well and good up until this point—life couldn't get any better, in fact. I was in law school—a pinnacle of education on the road to success. In conversations with my peers, we debated profound questions of justice, such as whether the right to a fox belonged to the hunter who began the pursuit or the hunter who captured it. We could debate this for hours. When I wasn't studying, I went surfing at Malibu's world-class point breaks. This good feeling followed me into the classroom. I went into midterm exams as I did any other exam I had taken as an undergrad—I knew how to write my way out of trouble when I didn't know the answers. I actually hoped for difficult questions because I could make my unrehearsed answers sound deep and I'd score well.

A couple of weeks later when I received the score back for my first exam, however, I was shocked. I didn't just barely fail it, I had bombed it. Worse, most of my midterms came back with similar results. Reality hit me upside the head—this would not be the breeze I had anticipated. Time seemed to freeze. My good life ground to a halt.

And then I received my fourth midterm grade. Bad news once again. Like a zombie, I walked back to my apartment. The door shut behind me and I fell apart. It wasn't the grade (thankfully, midterm exams are an exercise in preparation—only the final exam counts); it was that my entire view of myself now seemed to be hanging in the balance.

I thought I was a good student—was I?

I had thrown all my cards on the table—was I going to lose everything?

Everyone I knew was aware of what I was doing—could I tell them I didn't make it?

I had never failed at anything—would this be the first?

These are the kinds of questions that form who we think we are. When the core of who we believe we are is shaken, everything crumbles into sand.

I was in a dry, desolate place. Wandering in the desert, indeed.

I remembered that church sermon from a few months earlier when the preacher said, "We're led in and out of deserts throughout our lives." He explained that deserts come in different shapes and sizes: There are deserts in relationships—you're with someone you don't want to be with and you can't get out, or someone leaves you and you wonder why. There are deserts in careers—you realize that you went all in in one direction and you're not sure it was the right choice, or you find yourself in a career that you despise but you can't figure out what to do next. There are also internal deserts—you realize that you are not who you want to be, but you can't discern what you need to change. No matter the desert, we often wander until something makes us feel alive again.

I reflected back on the journey that brought me into this particular dry land. I had attended Bethel University in St. Paul, Minnesota, for my undergraduate education. Along with degrees in philosophy and business, I had had a great experience. Over the final two years, I had served as a resident adviser to two floors of freshman men, aced all my courses, and during the summers even found some success at competitive windsurfing. I felt that I was coming alive.

With everything going well and smoothly, I was not even the least bit intimidated or frightened about law school. It would be a breeze, I thought. I had a whole list of goals to check off, and

I was ready to take them on. Law school would be another easy one to complete. However, there's truth in Scripture's admonition that pride precedes a fall. Pride lets you miss a few turns in the car and I drove right into a desert.

How quickly we can become a prisoner of our expectations. With undergrad success behind me and facing a raft of low-scoring law-school midterms, I chained myself to the notion that I had to stick it out or be forever branded a failure. But what if I did make it through law school? At the end, would I be handcuffed to a life I would ultimately despise? For the first time in my life, the idea of simply disappearing seemed appealing.

I looked back to the stacks and stacks of books in the library behind me. Many students spent countless focused hours laboring over every single word in the thousands of books here. How could they focus so well? It's funny how a place built on academic freedom could feel so much like a prison.

I knew I needed to get back to work. But more than anything, I needed to be rescued.

A Moment to Remember

I skipped class.

I usually tried not to skip at all, but on this particular day, I found myself intrigued by a conference our law school was hosting. The conference featured lawyers who were going into the world's most dangerous places to help those in the greatest need. Something about it captured my imagination.

I slipped in the door and sat in the back row of the auditorium, as far from the front as possible, next to one of my classmates. I felt like a fish out of water. The people at the conference served the poor, volunteered their time, and went on mission trips. I hadn't done any of that.

The program started and a woman spoke about lawyers rescuing children from brothels, freeing slaves from brick factories, and releasing captives from illegal detention. I felt as though I was suddenly alone in the room. My heart beat fast. I felt as if I was watching myself in a movie—watching to see how I would react. The world seemed to be waiting for me to respond.

When the presentation ended, I sat there in silence. I turned to the person next to me.

"Wow," I said.

"Wow," she repeated back.

"I want to do this," I whispered.

"Me, too," she agreed.

I went home that night, pulled out my list of life goals, and scribbled, "Go and do something." I had a new box to check.

I struggled to fall asleep that night. I was too excited. I pictured myself doing the things that I had heard about. I imagined myself breaking down brothel doors and discovering prisons where kids were held illegally. What I had heard that day was heroic. I imagined myself as a hero to someone in the world. It didn't take superpowers—only the courage to go and do the things that others were afraid to do.

Not only was I drawn to the heroic, I reasoned that it would be good for me. I didn't know how, but I thought it might make me a better person.

Before I fell asleep, I dared myself to go.

I was ready to check my "go and do" box.

I didn't know it then, but I still had more wandering to do first.

Law is a great and noble profession, but I wasn't alive yet. It wasn't bringing me the kind of joy that woke me up in the morning before the alarm, and I wanted that. I knew many people, including lawyers, who loved what they did, but also many who did not. I felt that life was too short to take my chances and wind up on the wrong end of that spectrum.

Did that kind of joy actually exist? Maybe I was simply naive to believe that it did. Maybe that kind of joy was like winning the lottery—we hear just enough stories of those who hit the jackpot that we keep buying lottery tickets. Until then, maybe we are destined to wander most of our days. Could the prospects really be that bleak?

I kept thinking about the desert sermon. Maybe there was a reason for this frustration, for these sudden roadblocks. I thought back to that moment of inspiration and clarity I had felt in the auditorium. I imagined myself using my law degree to rescue people, finding them lost in prisons in the loneliest places in the world, or freeing them from slavery. I was heroic in my imagination, alive only when lost in thought.

For the next two years, I continued to think about that moment in the auditorium, but I found myself pulled in various directions by the things I "should" be doing instead. I picked up the pieces of my midterms and got the grades I needed. I found great internships and opportunities that took me on other courses—though never out of the desert. I was so consumed with surviving that my yearning to "go and do" took a back burner. And the box remained unchecked. It gnawed at me. I had yet to take myself up on my own dare.

But here I was, facing my last summer before studying for the bar exam and pursuing a career. It was now or never.

All conventional wisdom told me that to just go and do would be a bad career move and an even worse financial decision. "Summers should be spent getting an internship that becomes a job," I heard. Or, "How are you going to afford this?" And even "Why don't you wait until you graduate to try to save the world?"

Maybe they were right, I thought. I should really pursue a more traditional legal career. It was sensible; I made some phone calls. A respected, successful lawyer agreed to meet with me to discuss a job. We arranged an appointment.

Walking into the lawyer's office, I figured this was where I would end up for the summer—it would probably extend into the fall semester or even longer. I looked around the office: mahogany furniture, paneled doors, and a team to answer the phones. I sat down in a chair to get a feel for the place. If I got an opportunity here, how could I turn it down? This lawyer drove an exotic car, lived in a big house, and owned a private jet, no less. I pictured myself following in his footsteps and, one day, having my own private jet.

I was called into the lawyer's office. Escorted through a series of heavy oak doors, I sat down across from him. He told me all the things I could do to help him sell a business he owned—and the millions he might make from the sale. He grumbled that his last business didn't sell for a high enough price and that fuel prices were making it too costly to fly his jet. In spite of his success, he didn't seem joyful. Actually, he seemed really unhappy.

I broke into a cold sweat. My chest tightened and I could hear my heart beating in my head. I worried he could see the drops of sweat forming on my forehead. He asked if I could work on some projects for him—he'd pay me. This would be the beginning.

I stood on the mountaintop. I could see the riches and power below. I thought about my life list and the boxes I wanted to check. Some of the items I had placed on it years earlier were things money could buy, and now I could finally have them. Yet they no longer seemed to excite my imagination, a sharp contrast to the heroic "go and do" box.

I walked out of the office, wiped the sweat from my brow,

and never returned. I knew then that I had no choice but to risk everything. I finally had to accept my dare.

I immediately arranged an internship with an organization combating human trafficking and booked a ticket to Thailand for the summer. There was no turning back now.

Dare accepted.

CHAPTER 2

In over My Head

"THEY WANT ME TO DO WHAT?" I asked my fellow intern, Christina. "Outreach?!"

Only days before, I had left Los Angeles to make my way to Thailand. My "go and do" summer had begun. I was scheduled to do an internship with an anti–human-trafficking organization. I was supposed to help create a business model for employing and rehabilitating trafficking victims. I had big ideas and I had come to Thailand looking forward to implementing them. But what I heard at orientation on my first day spelled impending disaster: "outreach."

To my horror, they wanted all interns, including me, to do outreach. This meant spending my evenings in the red light district, building relationships with women and children on the street.

"This is not what I came here to do," I confessed to Christina. I came to Thailand to do big things. In the midst of earning my law degree and MBA, I couldn't waste a precious summer doing small things or, worse, nothing. To me, outreach sounded just like that: nothing.

"Well, maybe God has different plans for you," Christina replied. I wasn't so sure. This seemed more like a train wreck for my career. I sure couldn't see this being anything but a mistake.

Nonetheless, I went to do outreach that evening—begrudgingly, yet calmed by the fact that I planned to quietly bow out the next evening. As long as I tried it once, no one could complain, I reasoned. I would have given it a shot only to discover what I already knew—outreach was not my thing.

Outreach

The outreach team gathered for a meeting at a small coffee shop. I unenthusiastically glanced at my watch in regular intervals, wondering how long it would be before I could leave gracefully. A bell attached to the door jingled as a young Thai woman bounded in. Dressed in blue jeans and American brands, she could have been any Western college-aged girl. She cheerily greeted everyone—I suspected she attended regularly—and introduced herself simply as "Faa."

The outreach leaders presented me with a choice: I could go into the brothels to talk to the women, or I could play with the street children. Neither seemed profoundly appealing, yet the latter made me feel less uncomfortable. I picked the kids.

A surprised, almost scared look came over Faa's face. She coordinated outreach for the street children and would have to take me along. I could tell she wasn't sure about me. Before she could protest, however, the outreach leaders began praying and promptly dismissed us. We immediately hit the streets.

We rounded the corner into one of the largest red-light districts in the region, a hedonist's paradise. The street emitted a festive atmosphere as music blared from each of the bars. Colored lights poured out from every doorway. Some bars nearly burst at the seams with occupants, while others sat almost empty. From the main road, the red-light district was relatively hidden. Conveniently placed electrical transformers and opportunistic street vendors obscured a full view of the bars.

As we ventured down the street, the bars took on a stereotypical brothel image, sporting names like "Juicy" and "Delicious." Juicy played host to a dozen or more women sitting on chairs by the entrance waiting to be hired out for the evening. Their high-pitched siren call, "*Sawatdee kha*," nearly in unison, beckoned foreign men, who appeared to appreciate the attention and willingly accepted the invitation.

The customers consisted mostly of men with gray hair. I got the feeling these clients could be anyone: your next-door neighbor or high-school math teacher. The women appeared to be in their early twenties, but after a while, I realized that the average age was more like seventeen—likely even younger. The obvious and grotesque age difference between customer and client stood as an awkward contrast. The whole scene made me feel deeply uncomfortable. I wanted to turn around and walk away.

Instead, I followed Faa to a stoop across from the bars—two tile steps in front of a small convenience store, facing directly into one of the most popular brothels. Two older women already perched there took little notice of us initially. Faa greeted them in a language that didn't sound like Thai to me—it was more coarse and heavy, not the flowing tones of the Thai language.

The women looked weathered. Their dark skin showed deep, leathery lines. I guessed they lived difficult lives, laboring physically through many seasons of pulling rice under the blazing sun. In her hands, one woman clutched a bouquet of roses. The other woman cradled a dozen strings of small, sweet-smelling, white flower necklaces. The women appeared tired, as if they had walked all night long. I wondered what their lives were like.

Faa reached into her black canvas bag and pulled out a stack of books, games, and crayons. Like clockwork, two young girls came bounding up—one up the sidewalk and one from across the street. "P'Faa!" the girls yelled, running to Faa to give her a hug. They were thrilled to see her.

Faa introduced me to the young girls, Song and Pakpao, both about seven years old. Song unabashedly gave me a hug too. Each girl wore a beautiful ethnic dress; Song's was black and orange and adorned with the pattern and styling of a traditional hill tribe costume. The girls returned to Faa to dig into her treasure trove of crafts and games. Both tackled the coloring books and drawing paper with the intensity of children on Christmas morning. They crouched on the white tile steps, hovering over their books with fully focused attention.

More women and children continued gathering to join our veritable party. With bouquets of roses in their hands, they sat on the steps to converse among one another. Faa opened a plastic bag, revealing snacks and individual drink boxes of milk. She passed them out to the kids, who dove into the food with such force that I wondered when they had last eaten.

Another very young mother arrived. She was petite and pretty, most likely in her late teens. With a baby attached to her back by a strip of cloth, she stopped to untie the knot cinching her homemade baby carrier. Her baby appeared to have recently started walking—standing up, barely tottering a few feet, and then falling down.

For all these children, the street became a playground and everything on or near the sidewalk became a toy. A cockroach popped out of a nearby sewer grate and the new walker picked up the insect like a household pet. Her mother did not seem the least bit fazed. And, not a bottle of Purell in sight.

I started to piece together small bits of what had brought Faa out to the streets in the first place. I learned that she came from the same ethnic hill tribe as the kids we were playing alongside. There's a communal bond among the hill tribe groups, but Faa's presence seemed to revolve around something much deeper than ancestry. She told me about a night several years earlier when she had seen a five-year-old boy eating out of the trash. She could tell he was of the same hill tribe, so she approached him. He told her his story of abandonment and abuse. It broke her heart. She began paying, out of her own pocket, for the boy to attend school and live in a Christian children's home. I could tell his story wasn't far removed from Faa's own, but she wasn't ready to tell me everything yet.

One of the mothers stood up and signaled for her daughter, Noi, a four-year-old who had joined us. Reluctantly, after pleading to stay longer, Noi left her crayons and coloring books to work for her mother. The woman handed the little girl the flowers and, once again, they took to the streets. With that, the crowd began dissipating. Mothers rounded up their children and other kids who had been left on their own. Faa and I remained on the stoop next to the older women and watched them leave too.

Starting to reflect on all that I had seen, I turned to Faa.

"Why are they out here?" I asked.

"To sell flowers."

"The mothers make their kids sell flowers?"

"Yes."

"And some don't have parents?"

"No, not have parents."

"Huh. Where did they come from?"

"From village in the mountains."

"Do the kids go to school?"

"Some, yes. But most, no."

"Why did they come to Chiang Mai?"

"Earn money. The people are very poor and do not have land, so they can't make money."

"Will you ask them if they've sold any flowers?" I motioned toward two older women still sitting on the stoop.

"Yes." She turned to the woman next to her and they conversed in what I learned to recognize as the Akha language—a hill tribe tongue that is spoken, but not written. "Ah," Faa said after their long conversation. She looked away and paused, as if processing the whole story. A few seconds later, she turned to me. "Not a good night."

"How much do they sell on a good night?"

Faa continued the conversation and translated for me. "Maybe thirty *baht* on a bad night and one hundred *baht* on a good night." Thirty baht is about one dollar; one hundred baht is about three dollars. Each flower individually sells for ten baht, or about thirty cents.

"Can either woman read or write?"

Neither, Faa learned.

"Where do they live?"

This question led to a slightly longer dialogue between Faa and the woman. Faa told me that they lived in a small room near this street. Five families lived together in the one room.

"Would they let me come and visit them?"

The woman agreed without reservation, and Faa promised to take me sometime. About this time, the other outreach teams were coming back across the street. Two hours had gone by in what seemed like minutes. My outreach night was over.

As we started the walk back to the coffee shop parking lot to debrief, I couldn't help but wonder about everything I had seen that night. Why were girls as young as two years old out in this red-light district all night selling flowers? What prevented them from going to school? Why didn't their mothers find better employment opportunities? Why did the girls in the brothels choose this work? Did they even choose it? I was silent on the walk back as new questions continued to arise in my mind. I needed to find answers.

Something in my heart started to crack. With the coffee shop once again in view, I decided to break the vow I had made only hours earlier: I would return to outreach.

And go back I did—every night possible for the rest of the summer.

Like a surprise twist in the plotline, outreach evenings became my favorite nights of the week. All week, I looked forward to the opportunity to see the kids again. I wished every night were outreach.

If it wasn't an outreach night, I found ways to continue the work during the day. Whenever I could, I visited the kids, their families, and their homes. I learned that many of the kids didn't go to school. Not because they didn't want to, but because they didn't have birth certificates or identification. Many had crossed into Thailand from Burma at a very young age, brought by parents who sought migrant labor or fled the oppression. Thus, many kids lived in Thailand illegally but could not be recognized in Burma, either. Life was a state of limbo. I also learned that although selling flowers earned only a few dollars per night, those sales often accounted for their family's entire income. I soaked it all in like a sponge.

Everything I learned challenged me, and I couldn't stop thinking about it. It hurt to see the kids living in horrible conditions. I started to share their burden. I started to come alive.

Any given night brought unexpected blessings. One night, a four-year-old girl with bouncing pigtails rounded the corner onto the main street lined with brothels. "Noi!" I shouted, jumping to my feet from the stoop across the street. Noi looked at me, and then froze. A mischievous grin broke across her face and she suddenly sprinted into a bar. A dozen roses in her hands, she circled the bar tables, keeping her eyes on me the whole time, paying no attention to the customers to whom she was supposed to sell the flowers. Running out of the bar, she threw the roses to her mother and leapt from the curb into my arms. She looked up at me with a huge grin of excitement, and I knew my presence was meaningful to her. I wished I could take her away from here—off this street. Even if only for this one cherished moment, the entire summer would be worth it.

The evenings also brought unanticipated twists as I made new friends. One evening, a teenage girl holding a giant bouquet of roses wandered up to talk to Faa. Faa introduced her as Faifah. Faifah was a beautiful fourteen-year-old girl, thin with high cheekbones and a sweet smile. She was a tiny girl, but her voice was deep and husky. I would never have guessed she was a girl on the street. Her bubbly personality was contagious—the kind of girl who might be voted most likely to succeed in high school, if only she could attend one.

Faifah's mother had carried her across the border into Thailand when she was very young. Her mother subsequently went missing through unknown circumstances, though many claimed she was found drunk on the street and deported. Faifah didn't know whether she was still alive. Thus, Faifah had grown up alone on Thailand's streets. She slept where she could, often staying with friends. Her beauty and age made her a target for abusive men. Every day was tenuous.

Faifah sat and giggled with Faa, like girls talking in a high school hallway. Faifah's happy, energetic personality never suggested her sad circumstances—her family's whereabouts unknown, she left to sell flowers to tourists and sleep wherever she could find a place to lay her head. In her husky voice, Faifah spoke a few words to me in English that she had picked up through life on the streets—"bar English," they call it. She sang me a beautiful song in her native tongue, and then laughed as she told me I should be her older brother. I figured she could use one—so I proudly accepted the honor. Little did I know what that was going to mean.

The Least of These

By the time summer was over, I had bonded with nearly a dozen children. I collectively referred to them as "my kids." We couldn't speak in the same tongue, yet we all spoke one universal language: play. I was seeing firsthand how easy it is to encounter God through those we consider the least of humanity. Matthew 25:35-40 says that what you do for "the least of these," you do for God:

> "I was hungry, and you fed me. I was thirsty, and you gave me a drink. I was a stranger, and you invited me into your home. I was naked, and you gave me clothing. I was sick, and you cared for me. I was in prison, and you visited me."
>
> Then these righteous ones will reply, "Lord, when did we ever see you hungry and feed you? Or thirsty and give you something to drink? Or a stranger and show you

hospitality? Or naked and give you clothing? When did we ever see you sick or in prison and visit you?"

And the King will say, "I tell you the truth, when you did it to one of the least of these my brothers and sisters, you were doing it to me!"

These street kids were "the least of these." But when I served them, I felt that I was serving God directly. The song "Heaven" by Live scored my summer. The band sings of God's revelation through relationships and nature. The line "I don't need no one to tell me 'bout heaven, I look at my daughter and I believe" played repeatedly in my head, taking on a deeper meaning than I had understood before. When I looked at these kids—"my kids"—I didn't just feel God, I *saw* God.

The reality of a boarding pass for my return flight soon hit me. I didn't want to leave. It wasn't so much that I wanted to stay in Thailand but that I didn't want to leave the kids. I could see the brothels across the street, and I knew they really had no choices. I couldn't bear the idea that I might return in ten years to find these kids in the brothels—not when I could help do something now to prevent it.

Stepping onto the Jetway, I realized my summer had originally been about me. I wanted to come to Thailand—it would be an adventure; I'd check my "go and do" box, and I might even become a better person. But then, by God's grace and to my initial chagrin, it had become completely *not* about me. It wasn't at all the experience I'd expected or the résumé builder I'd anticipated. Nor was I the person I'd hoped to become.

That summer had been about so much more than me. It was all about a street and some kids who called it home. It was about the last thing I ever expected I'd be doing. Yet in a different sense, at the end of the summer, it was back to being about me. How could I get on that plane, never return, and go about the rest of my life?

If anything were to change—on this street or anywhere—it had to come through an individual making a choice. If I wanted to see something change, it was up to me. I couldn't wash my hands of it assuming someone else would pick up the slack.

I didn't want to be another volunteer who came and then left. I didn't want to be a person who posts photos online of me hugging kids I couldn't even name. I wanted to remain present in the lives of "my kids," even if I was physically on the other side of the world. Too much had happened. I felt invested and determined that I would keep the relationships alive.

When I returned to the States, I wrote letters to the kids and asked Faa to deliver them. I didn't expect a reply. Could they or their parents understand the mail system? But one afternoon a month later, an envelope showed up in my mailbox. Seven-year-old Song had sent me a drawing and a picture of herself. I was touched. I had no idea how she accomplished this, but Faa had helped send the letter to me. Holding the letter, I felt, once again, God's presence. Now, it was on—she had pushed back.

I wrote more letters to the kids. Most of the time, I never heard back, but Faa did tell me that they received the letters and wanted to know why I had left. I wanted to do more. I inquired into Song's education and whether we could get her off the street. Coincidentally, her mother didn't have the money to send Song to school the next year and didn't know what she would do. Through Faa, I relayed a message to Song's mother. I asked first what her mother's dream was for her daughter. Her mother replied that she hoped Song could go to college, maybe study in the US, and that she would use her life to help other people. I told Song's mother that I wanted to help. I hoped Song could go to college, too, and said I would try to make sure she was able to do so, but her mother needed to make sure Song no longer worked on the street, that she made good choices, and that she stayed in school. In other words, the next time I visited that street, I did not want to find Song there selling flowers. Song's mom agreed and was very grateful.

Over the next few months, Faa and I strategized about how we could get Song into a school. Faa visited nearly every school in the city, but most of the state-run schools wouldn't take anyone without official identification. Finally, Faa found an excellent Christian school that understood the situation and would take her without immediate ID. The school was one of the best in the city and sent many of its students to college. A year's tuition was only $500, including uniforms.

After Song started school, we began working on Song's birth certificate and ID. Through a rather lengthy process of filing legal papers, she obtained an ID that allowed her to stay in school. Her mother kept her end of the bargain and took her off the streets—she never sold flowers again.

Yet, Song's home situation—awful conditions as well as her mother's abusive boyfriend—was far less than ideal. Faa found a Christian dormitory for Song to stay in so that she did not have to live in tract housing—padlocked storage closets turned into rooms for unauthorized migrants—housing subsequently condemned. The dorm became a place where Song could thrive in a healthy environment and be encouraged to further her education.

I like to think that we didn't merely provide an education, but that we also played a small role in saving Song's life. It's amazing how an unintentional meeting on the street could alter the trajectory of both our lives. Without our meeting and bond, I sometimes wonder whether Song would have ended up across the street in the brothels one day.

For me, however, my unplanned meeting with Song sent my life spiraling into confusion. What was I supposed to do? Playing a small part in saving a life was fulfilling, but what was I supposed to do next? And what about the other people I had met? All I could think about was getting back to see my kids again. Song was in a good place, but Noi and Faifah were still vulnerable. Most of the kids that grew up on the street eventually ended up in the brothels or as very young mothers in abusive situations. I had heard even more horrific stories of children being abducted for days by abusive foreigners who prey on street kids. Very few made it off the street unscathed. I couldn't do much from the United States except pray for them and for an opportunity to return.

CHAPTER 3

Losing Faifah

IT HAD BEEN NINE MONTHS since I had left Thailand, and I thought about the kids every day. With graduation only a few weeks away, the bar exam breathing down my neck, and no job lined up, I didn't know whether I would ever go back.

In April 2008, I received an e-mail from Faa saying that something bad had happened. I called her in Thailand that night. Faifah had been deported to Burma, she said. Police had caught her without identification during a raid one evening. The police had driven down the street where they sold flowers with a truck and rounded up every child they could find. Faifah spent nearly two weeks being passed between holding jails as she awaited an unknown fate. Although Faifah had not chosen to come to Thailand in the first place, it had become the place she called home. She had no home in Burma.

At the border, we would learn later, the barbed-wire-enclosed wagon had backed up to the border of Burma, and the border patrol marched Faifah across the bridge. Burma might be the last place anyone would want to be dropped off, especially a fifteen-year-old girl. Faifah stood bewildered, suddenly tossed into one of the world's most dangerous places, where everything revolves around the black market.

Faifah hitchhiked into the mountains until she arrived at her ancestral village, a small community she knew only by name. The small bamboo hut in which she had been born was nestled among the other small huts on the mountainside. She asked around to learn if her family still lived there.

Faifah's mother and father were shocked when she approached their hut. Not only was Faifah alive, but she had found her way back to her childhood home. Faifah was equally surprised that her mother and father were both alive. The reunion, however, did not last long. Faifah's mother sensed opportunity. In Burma, having a daughter can be like winning the lottery. On the first night at a brothel, a young girl can fetch as much as one thousand dollars. For Faifah's family, who were surviving on less than a dollar a day, a daughter could supply many years' worth of wages.

When it came time for her mother to make the sale to a brothel agent, Faifah escaped from her village and fled back to the Thailand border. Under the cover of night, she swam the river dividing Thailand and Burma, scampering back up the riverbank and into safety. She found a truck driver willing to allow her to hide in the back as he drove to the city. Two hours down the road, immigration officers flagged the truck down at a checkpoint and searched it. Faifah once again found herself arrested and back in jail.

In the outside world, we knew little of what was happening until word of Faifah's second arrest made its way to Faa. As soon as I heard the news, I alerted various antitrafficking agencies on the ground and everyone I could identify who might be able to help. Sadly, most seemed indifferent—it's one girl, and it would be too difficult to do anything, they said. I found that answer unacceptable. Faifah had declared me her brother, and I wouldn't let her go that easily. "Simply go to the jail, tell her that we're working on it, and that we care for her," I pleaded. Finally, we found someone willing to do at least that, but it was too late—she had already been deported.

This time, arriving back in Burma, Faifah truly had nowhere to turn. She walked along the road toward the edge of town, then followed a foot trail into the jungle. On the edge of town, Faifah spotted a dilapidated Buddhist shrine. The simple, abandoned, concrete structure appeared barely visible amid the thickening forest. Faifah approached and put her back against the cold wall. She slumped to the ground and began to sob. When she opened her swollen eyes, she realized that she was no longer alone. The next few days marked some of Faifah's darkest hours. Now in the company of drifters who possessed no respect for her dignity, she was drugged and raped repeatedly.

Faifah's situation did not go unnoticed for long. The small trail that brought her to the shrine continued to wind its way from the city and into the foothills. At the end of the path stood a small Christian orphanage operated by a pastor and his wife. Passing by the area a few times each day, the pastor's wife spotted the young girl, newly arrived and in hostile circumstances. Sensing trouble, she approached Faifah, offering refuge and a place to stay. Faifah readily accepted.

To the outside world, Faifah had fallen off the grid. She could easily disappear into Burma, never to be reached again. We waited. We worried. We prayed. We waited some more. Still nothing. It appeared as though Faifah might be another statistic—a girl gone missing. It was the kind of story you hear about but never know anyone who has experienced it. This time, I knew someone. Two months passed with no news. Finally, one day Faifah called Faa from a mobile phone in Burma to say that she was alive and living in an orphanage. We rejoiced.

Into the Desert Yet Again

I was in the desert yet again. I wanted to "go and do," but try as I might, no doors opened. I applied to many places and even considered working abroad for free for a year. We wander in and out of deserts, my pastor had said, and I clearly had wandered back into one.

As I thought through my postgraduation options, I received a phone call about a meeting with a partner in a major law firm. A position with the firm started at $120,000 per year, not including a year-end bonus.

I stood, once again, on the highest mountain. The world below reminded me of the material things I had always wanted. I thought about the beautiful lofts in the downtown warehouse district. I thought about the office towering above the city skyline. I thought about the ski boat with a slip on the lake.

Then I thought about my kids in Thailand who could not afford school, and for the first time in my life, the boat seemed to be of little importance.

I watched some of my friends struggle with the same question. As they faced the prospect to "go and do," they identified career opportunities that brought them deep gladness. However, when they stood on the mountain, the riches of the world were too hard to decline and they walked away from their chance for joy. I saw other friends hold firm and eventually find the right opportunity, even though many of them wandered through the desert for a while to get there.

I thought about my journey and the journey that my friends at law school had taken. I saw how one summer had changed my life, and I knew other students wanted the same thing. I wanted to create an environment where the personal revolution could take place, where students could "go and do" and come alive. I wanted to share the I'm-hearing-something-that's-changing-my-life moment that I'd had in the auditorium. As much as I wanted to return to Thailand more permanently, my gut told me I could do more than fulfill my own desire. I could go out as one person helping the world, or I could build a movement to help send many across the globe. At Pepperdine, we had a fledgling initiative spearheaded by students like me. My summer cast a vision in me for what I and the dozens just like me could do who felt the yearning to "go and do." Thailand, of course, was part of that vision.

As I was standing in the administrative office at our law school one day, an assistant to the dean asked what I really wanted to do. I told her a few of the positions I wanted—including relocating to Thailand—but admitted, shyly, that if I could wave a magic wand, I might stay and build my vision for the Global Justice Program at Pepperdine.

"You'd be great at that," Lorraine said, looking at me sincerely and intently. "Are you asking them?"

"No," I chuckled. "I don't think the deans would consider it."

"How do you know?"

"Well, I guess I don't, but there's not an open position."

"It never hurts to try," Lorraine petitioned. "What have you got to lose?"

I started to feel nervous. My idea was bold, but putting bold dreams into action can be terrifying. I'd be vulnerable. I could fail. It might be like that first year of law school all over again. I wanted certainty and comfort, not risk and, possibly, another desert. Yet she convinced me to make an appointment. I couldn't back out.

A few days later I met with the dean, Kenneth W. Starr. Dean Starr was one of the top constitutional scholars in the United States; he'd argued dozens of cases in front of the US Supreme Court and served as solicitor general, among many other high profile positions. Whenever I had met with him in the past, I always made sure I was prepared, but I had never asked him for anything of this magnitude.

I walked into Dean Starr's office and I told him my vision—a bold vision for the Global Justice Program. We would build a global initiative focusing on plugging our students into gaps where justice and rule of law fail those in desperate need. I set out the goals I wanted to achieve, and I asked him to hire me. He looked at me stoically, taking occasional notes, and gave no indication of whether he approved or disapproved.

"Let me think about this," he said at the end of our conversation. I imagined it was a nice way to let me down easy. I left the office happy that I had tried exhausting all options.

Four months later, I still had no job. I had not heard from Dean Starr. My last final exam rapidly approached, to be followed by a week of graduation pomp and circumstance. Graduating without any job prospects loomed on the horizon.

One day as I was crossing through the law school atrium between classes, I happened to run into the dean. He asked me to come by his office, since we had not yet closed the loop on our conversation. But, he emphasized, I should wait until after my last final. Mercifully, I suspected, he would give me the bad news after my finals so that I wouldn't be distracted.

With my finals concluded, I assumed I would be going home—back to the Midwest. I scouted a rental trailer.

I figured I would use my meeting with Dean Starr as an

entrée to other jobs. He could open doors, make a phone call on my behalf, or write a recommendation letter. I prepped a black-leather portfolio with current job opportunities at various law firms and international organizations. After he told me no, I planned to open the folder and spring these opportunities on him. If he couldn't offer me a job, he might feel more obligated to help me find one.

Wearing a dark suit and red tie, I waited outside the office for a prior meeting to conclude. I walked into the dean's office as I had just months before. We sat down in the same chairs. Across the same coffee table. We exchanged brief formalities about finals and the impending bar exam.

"So, about your Global Justice Program proposal."

My fingers clasped the edge of the portfolio. I was ready to transition effortlessly into how he could help me get my second-tier jobs.

"Let's do it," Dean Starr said affirmatively. "We'll work out the details later."

I was shocked. I had a job.

Finding Faifah

I had no job description.

For someone like me who prefers blank slates upon which to grow big ideas, it was a dream come true. At the meeting where Dean Starr hired me, I asked him what he wanted me to do. His reply? Bring the most inspiring people in, and send the most motivated students out. Just as I'd been inspired to "go and do," this was a proposition to which I could relate.

With no staff and little idea what I was doing, I began building a network with blue-chip, faith-based organizations and inviting the most inspiring justice seekers to Pepperdine. The response was overwhelming. With our students, it seemed as though we might have opened a floodgate. My experience searching for something fulfilling was a shared, collective experience. It captivated imaginations.

Yet one important task remained at the forefront of my mind: find Faifah.

A couple of weeks into the job, I met with Dean Starr to make another request. I had important business in Thailand. I told him about Faifah, my kids, various organizations with which we could partner, and a spring break service trip I wanted to lead.

He pursed his lips, rubbed his chin, and paced around the room. A few seconds later, he looked up at me and said, "Good."

I walked out of the office and booked tickets for Thailand. I was going home.

Two weeks later, somewhere 37,000 feet above the cold waters separating Alaska and Russia, I started to second-guess myself. Sometimes I have audacious travel ideas that seem perfectly sound in the abstract, but when it comes to execution, I wonder what I was thinking.

By the time our wheels touched down at our final destination, I'd flown nearly twenty-four hours and had gone without sleep for closer to thirty-six. Yet stepping out of the terminal felt like home again—the sights, the smells, the feelings. Still, with a rental car waiting and a six-hour drive to Burma ahead, this seemed like much less of a good idea now. The drive, tiring and arduous, had me, once again, questioning my good judgment.

Faa met me at the airport. She'd be my guide and translator. She arranged for the rental car, but had never driven one herself—only motorbikes—so the piloting was up to me. Our car was a tiny, bright-red two door, the cheapest car I could get. A small car didn't help much, though. Everything was reversed and confusing, with the driver on the right, and road signs in

Thai. I almost ran into another car in the airport parking lot. And I continually turned on wipers when I intended to signal.

More than anything, I wanted to sleep, or at least rest a bit. However, if we were to see Faifah, this was our only window in Faa's schedule and my busy trip. We had to get on the road immediately, with night arriving soon. Exhaustion and confusion made for a long drive.

About three quarters into our six-hour drive, we passed through a small mountain village. Suddenly, a pack of stray dogs darted out in front of us. I couldn't stop, and there was nowhere to swerve. I held the steering wheel tightly.

After a thud, followed by two bangs, I saw a dog tumbling down the street behind us in my rearview mirror. I pulled the car over. I was surprised at how little damage had been done. The dog was nowhere to be found.

Faa held her stomach with a horrified look on her face. She couldn't speak.

We got back in the car and drove off. We were silent for a few minutes.

"I feel really bad about that dog," I said. "It was still walking, so hopefully it lived."

"It's okay," Faa replied. "Someone will come and take it to make dinner."

Uh, what? The closer we got to the Burma border, the more I knew we were in a place that played by different rules.

The next morning we arrived at the Thai-Burma border. I stamped out of Thailand and walked across the bridge—no man's land—to Burma's checkpoint. A mustard-yellow customs office guards the entrance to this remote country. Uniformed officers guided me into a tiny building where an old bedsheet served as a door. Inside, I begrudgingly surrendered my passport to the military junta in control of one of the world's most dangerous countries. Watching my passport disappear into a desk was one of the most unsettling feelings I ever experienced—I had let go of my last bit of safety. In exchange, I received a temporary paper visitor's permit.

The world in Burma is different—night and day—like walking back one hundred years through a time warp. This border town is the Wild West. Its commerce hub is the thriving black market, where one can buy anything from fake cigarettes to counterfeit Gucci handbags to poached leopard pelts. The country is one of the world's largest producers of opiates and a haven for human trafficking. Chaos was everywhere.

With our first steps onto Burmese pavement, we were swarmed by a crowd of panhandlers, beggars, and souvenir peddlers. I put my hand on my wallet as we pushed our way through the throng of people to find a motorcycle-taxi driver who had heard of the orphanage.

Our motorcycle taxi—a seemingly homebuilt, fire-engine-red three-wheeler that inspired little confidence—rattled out of town. Every hill presented a challenge, squeezing every last ounce of torque from the taxi's gears. At one point, I offered to step out to reduce weight. The driver waved for me not to get off.

The small city on the border disappeared among rolling rural hills dotted with tiny villages. Finally, we pulled up to the base of a large hill, on the top of which was Faifah's orphanage. The driver turned off the engine.

"Pii Jay! Pii Faa!" Faifah's voice shrieked, recognizing us. Faifah ran down the hill with tears filling her eyes. Her baggy, ragged clothes barely fit her. When she reached me, she gave me the biggest hug. She still had her beautiful smile and, despite all that she had been through, the same sparkle in her eyes. She giggled at nearly everything I said to her.

I spent the day with Faifah, seeing where she lived, where she slept, and what she ate. Simplicity abounded. At one point, Faifah showed me her small mattress in a room shared with many of the other orphans. She spread out all her possessions before me on her bed—I was shocked to see that almost everything she owned consisted of the small gifts I had mailed her for Christmas—a blanket, a hairstyling kit, and a stuffed animal.

At the end of the day, I asked Faifah what her dreams were, what she wanted to be. Faifah thought for a moment and replied, "I just want to work." She simply wanted to feel that she was a part of something bigger.

After spending the afternoon with Faifah and the other kids at the orphanage, we walked back to the border. Faifah joined us. We walked through the jungle and past the wicked cement shrine. I looked away as I passed the evil vagrants hovering around the shrine. Faifah grabbed my arm and put it across her shoulders. She still needed a brother. I thought back to the night I had met this innocent girl. A lot had happened in a short time, and I imagined how much more might take place before I would see Faifah again. She was in a good place, a safe place. Maybe this would end happily after all.

Searching for Faifah

A year after the visit to find Faifah, I was back in Asia once again. Two months after I left her at the orphanage, she had disappeared. I didn't know why and I didn't know what had happened to her. No one knew. But when she finally resurfaced, I made another trip to see her.

Faa joined me as a guide and called Faifah, who now apparently owned her own mobile phone, and told her to meet us at the border. Once again, I made the treacherous six-hour, white-knuckle drive via rental car, and crossed the same border into

Burma, while experiencing the same fear as I again surrendered my passport.

Across the border, I parted the sea of swarming panhandlers, keeping an eye out for the young girl who had not been heard from for a year. She was waiting there, just beyond the red motorbike taxis. Faifah was no longer the innocent girl in ragged clothes I had left in the orphanage, but a modern girl with bright red nails, a trendy haircut, and knockoff designer jeans. The transformation was striking.

After a few moments of celebration, she motioned for us to follow her. We crossed the street, then went into an alley and behind the buildings that lined the main road. We stepped into another world—a crowded market that sold anything I could ever imagine. We darted through the rows of stalls and into streets that were now far off the beaten path. Locals gave me strange looks—as if they wondered what I was doing there. I started to get a bit nervous.

Faifah stopped at a small wooden stall. She seemed to know the owner. He pulled out two mopeds. Faifah hopped on one and Faa and I on the other. I didn't know where we were going that would require a moped, but I hesitantly followed.

"Faa, what's happening?" I asked. She didn't know.

We drove through many city blocks, then out of the city limits—farther than the Burma government, which tightly controls movement, probably wanted me to go. We drove through a burning landfill, an area that looked like the Apocalypse had happened. Smoke rose from the ground, and a great cloud of ash covered the road. The landfill was dotted with makeshift shacks of the poorest Burmese people who lived in the dump. We drove farther, through a great field of logs piled up from the junta's clear-cutting operations. We passed Buddhist shrines and tiny villages. As we moved farther and farther from civilization, I wondered where we were going and if I could get back.

Faifah finally pulled onto a small path into the trees and stopped just before a steep hill. Once through the initial trees, I could tell we were in a tiny hill-tribe village. I had no idea where we were, and I was certain this place wasn't on any map. We walked up a steep hill and past a series of small bamboo huts. We finally stopped in front of the highest hut on the hill. Faa took a seat on the ground while I stood in the ready position, still unsure of what was happening. I had no idea where I was, though I knew that I couldn't get back to the border from here if I tried. Faa told me everything was fine, but she didn't know what it was like to be the tall white American who stood out like a sore thumb. Faifah went inside the hut, returning with her mother, the same woman who had once tried to sell Faifah.

What am I doing here? My thoughts started racing. I could disappear without a trace and no one would ever know. I imagined someone, like Faifah's mother, trying to extort money from me before I crossed the border again. With that, my stomach knotted up. I thought about the money I had spent on flights, hotels, and rental cars to find myself in this precarious position. My heart rate climbed higher. But then I gazed back into the face of Faifah. I remembered that I had come for her, and my fear dissipated.

Faifah handed me a fresh chicken egg and giggled. Her beautiful smile reminded me that, deep down, she was still the same young girl I'd met on the streets a couple of years earlier. The egg was warm, and Faifah found it particularly funny to point that out to me. She showed me around her parents' bamboo hut. The small bamboo shack seemed more like a shack for storing rice than a traditional Akha house. The simple single room inside had a raised platform for sleeping on one side and a charcoal fire pit on the other, with no division between bedroom and kitchen. We stepped back outside and Faifah sat down next to her mother on the porch. They appeared to be on better terms now.

I thought about what had brought Faifah and me to the point where our lives intersected in such a significant way. A lot had happened that I couldn't explain. We met on the street in a red-light district—a street where I hadn't wanted to be, but where Faifah had dared me to be her older brother. I had accepted the challenge, never thinking where it might take me. Faifah had been arrested, nearly trafficked, abused, and forgotten by most of the world. I had returned to find her—twice now.

I asked Faifah to fill in the gaps of the last year. She explained how she had left the orphanage to provide for her parents, bowing to the cultural pressure to care for one's elders. Yes, the same unemployed, drunken mother who had tried to sell Faifah the year before was now Faifah's dependent. Yet Faifah was ecstatic—she finally had the opportunity to work. "I serve in restaurant," she explained. Even more, she had a room to live in at the restaurant. She simply desired to work, to show her family that she could provide for them. And she desperately, proudly wanted to show us where she worked. We agreed to go and see.

After some time with her parents and lunch in the village, we boarded the motorbikes to head back into town. The motorcycle ride back into the border town ended at a white stand-alone building—her restaurant, Faifah explained. She ushered us inside and up a flight of stairs. The second floor opened into a long hallway with numbered doors. Faifah opened one—"her room." The room was filled with young girls sleeping side by side on reed mats. She closed the door as a matron stepped up behind us, commenting on how Faifah brought in so many men. Today it was me, I gathered. My stomach knotted up.

I knew what this place was—a Burmese brothel. I looked at Faa—I could tell she was sad. She spoke very little and wanted to leave quickly. I felt a little panicked, actually.

Once again, I was overwhelmed by the same question: "What am I doing here?" I decided my time in Burma was over and wanted to get back across the border as quickly as possible.

Faifah's story had turned to what I hoped none of the kids I had met would face. Left with what seemed to be no choice and no one to fight for her, she had fallen victim to the evil pressures and circumstances facing uneducated, vulnerable young women in Burma.

Saying good-bye at the border, I knew that I couldn't solve Faifah's problems, I couldn't solve the problems in Burma, and I couldn't solve the problem of human trafficking. I had had many conversations with organizations and government bodies about trafficking in Burma—it was a complex and dangerous situation. That didn't mean we shouldn't try to help, but change wouldn't happen overnight. In this very instance, I could only give Faifah a hug. Was I okay with that?

Faifah needed to know that someone cared about her—that she was important enough for someone to fly eight thousand miles simply to see her—and she did. She needed to know that she was worth the risk and worth the cost, that for her, all was not lost. I'm inclined to try to solve things, but not all situations lend themselves to ready-made solutions. Nonetheless, I knew that I had been called to show up where no one else would, when no one else would. In these places, I had been called to be the hands and feet of God.

We all have moments of self-reflection in our lives where we ask, "What am I doing here?" You can answer the question one of two ways: "I don't know, and I don't like it," or "I'm right where I need to be." When I held the warm chicken egg and gazed off into the jungle, then back at Faifah, I knew I was right where I needed to be. I was living a story Jesus wanted me to tell. And the theme of that story was rescue: my own rescue, by the stirring call to go and do something. In this case, that something was Faifah's rescue, if only from the fear that no one else in this world cared.

CHAPTER 4

It's Not about Changing the World

I'VE BEEN BACK TO THAILAND so many times now that I've lost count. One of my great joys is getting to visit Song, watch her grow up, and keep our relationship alive. Meeting her first on the street and seeing the enormous transition she has made up to now is a beautiful thing. She's learning English, so every time I visit her, we communicate a little better and learn more about each other.

She continues to excel in school and has since moved in with a wonderful new "go and do" family. They moved to Thailand with their two high-school-aged children to start a home where they could take in children who were in vulnerable and abusive situations. Their home is a small family—and they want to keep it that way. Song is safe there and, most important, she's happy. Knowing that I played a small role in helping stop something terrible makes our visits that much richer to me.

I continue to keep in touch with Faifah as best I can, as she cycles through falling off the radar and resurfacing. I pray that she finds herself in a better situation, much like Song did. Although Faifah's story doesn't yet have a happy ending, it doesn't stop me from continuing to fight for her and other kids like her. On the contrary, it reinforces the importance of the issues. In my case, I have dived deeper into the problem of stateless children in the region. I'm constantly exploring long-range, strategic opportunities to find solutions. This is my parallel career.

Six years ago, I sat alone in the back of an auditorium. Today, at any Global Justice event we host, the room is packed with students experiencing that same this-is-my-moment feeling. From undergrads to graduate students, if an opportunity is available, all hands raise in a chorus of "Send me!"

It's part of a groundswell, a forming wave of the desire to "go and do" as an expression of faith. It's a desire to live the stories that Jesus taught us and play a small role in God's greater story arc. Maybe it's helping obtain a life-changing slip of paper identification, or maybe it's showing up in a near hopeless situation to give a single hug. Whatever it may be, it's a desire to make a tiny part of the world a better place.

Many days, I still wonder what, if anything, I'm contributing. It's certainly not all high impact trips to dangerous locations. That's only a very small part of it. Most of the work is less than glamorous.

When I'm back in the States in my office, I never know what my day will look like. Some days are exciting: meetings with cabinet-level ministers, interacting with the greatest practitioners in global justice, or planning sessions for our next strategic operation on the ground in Africa. Other days are less exciting: I am often buried in paperwork and e-mail or I'm preparing proposals for donors or I'm working with my team on the latest research project. The majority of my time is spent purely communicating—externally with our partners and internally with those I work with at Pepperdine.

Nonetheless, I always know one thing for sure: many students will come to my office—the door is always open.

"Well, I'd like to talk to you about what I'm going to do after graduation," Brady the Revolutionary says as he drops his bag on the floor and plops down onto the couch. With his signature Vietnam-era army jacket and unkempt beard, he might feel more at ease in a dimly lit coffee shop than in my office. He looks like the leader of a guerrilla army.

"I've really been thinking about it a lot, and I feel a need to leave the country for a while."

Brady is one of those guys that when he tells me he's been thinking, I know he's been thinking. He's a philosopher at heart, though he didn't realize it until he was too deep into another major.

"Great. Tell me more." I spin around in my desk chair, turning my attention from e-mail to Brady. "Why do you feel like this is what you want to do?"

"I think I'd like to work somewhere really outside my comfort zone —maybe India. I've been drawn to India, or the former Yugoslavia. I feel like I've always lived really comfortably, and I need to challenge myself."

As we talk further, I get the sense that this personal crisis is more about challenging his faith. Brady intellectualizes faith to the point where all roads converge. He's come to that place where there's a strong argument and an intelligent, respected thinker behind nearly every theological position. It's at this point where Brady's faith needs to go for a ride to see what it really means to him personally.

I see a little bit of myself in Brady. He reminds me of what

I went through in law school. Brady grew up in a solid Christian family, attended church regularly, and got into an excellent undergrad program at Pepperdine. Below the surface, Brady is at the same inner tipping point that I was: he's in the desert, facing both a crisis of self and a crisis of faith. He needs something to truly challenge him and challenge his faith. Though he's nearing the end of his formal education, Brady can feel that he still has something more to learn.

Are You Trying to Change the World?

When it comes to our desire to go and do, the first thing we must realize is that it's not about changing the world. Instead, it's about changing ourselves. And the great thing is that if we allow God to change us, then along the way, he allows us to change the lives of those we encounter. It always starts with us—with God working in us.

When I first got involved with global justice work, people often accused me of wanting to change the world. I never said it myself; it always came from other people. Whenever I heard it, no matter how I heard it, the phrase always troubled me. I found the comments deprecating or exaggerated, portraying me as either a naive young idealist or as someone who has accomplished something really significant. I was neither. I wasn't trying to save old trees by sitting high in their branches to confound loggers. Nor was I doing anything that could ever nominate me for a Nobel Peace Prize. I simply did what I thought should be done when I looked at the world.

I believe that the old cliché actually holds us back. At times, I tried to simply accept the phrase and use it, but I couldn't. It felt arrogant. It wasn't me. If I ever did try to change the world, I knew I would either completely fail, become a cynic who continually complained that nothing would ever change, or I'd get so caught up in an obscure project that I'd one day be found leading a cult of indigenous tribal people in the jungle, like Kurtz in *Heart of Darkness.*

On the other end of the spectrum, it's easy to get caught up in the idea that we have to accomplish something of extreme significance. And we believe that this is fulfilled only by some momentous, sweeping action. We celebrate human achievement to a degree where anything less seems devoid of purpose. We might ask, If no one celebrates what we're doing, are we doing anything worthwhile?

Brady the Revolutionary never mentioned fixing any global problem or saving anyone's life. For that matter, he never mentioned anything external. Brady talked only about changing himself. He wanted to serve an organization that helped people and maybe make the world a better place through his time there. If there was a revolution that Brady was leading, it was his own personal one.

Brady's revolution mirrored my own. That moment in the auditorium was about nothing more than me. It certainly had nothing to do with changing the world. Rather, it was a crisis of self and faith. I wanted to challenge myself. I had realized two things about myself: first, I was living a pretty comfortable life, and second, it's a big world out there. When these two understandings finally collided, I found myself in crisis.

For each person, the solution to this crisis is a personal revolution.

The Personal Revolution

Gandhi is commonly quoted as saying, "Be the change you wish to see in the world." I've seen this phrase listed on countless Facebook profiles, bumper stickers, and dorm room bulletin boards. I like it, too, but it never made my list of words to live by because I've always wondered exactly what Gandhi meant. For the longest time I read the quote as a call to action. I interpreted it as, "If you want it done right, then go do it yourself." I thought Gandhi expected me to change the world, and that seemed like a bigger request than I could match.

I wanted to read the context in order to properly interpret it. Maybe he meant something different. What if we weren't using it as he intended? I looked it up. Or, at least, I tried. I learned that the quote does not appear in any of Gandhi's writings or captured speeches. As the story goes, after Gandhi finished a prayer service, those in attendance immediately asked him how they were supposed to change when the world hasn't changed. "The world needs to change first," they lamented. So Gandhi said something to the effect that "the world will not change if we do not change."

Arun Gandhi, Mahatma Gandhi's grandson, is the only one known to have heard Gandhi make this statement. It's not clear whether the famous quote came word for word or saw some finessing befitting the bumper sticker market, but it certainly has Gandhi's spirit. Arun Gandhi described the ensuing dialogue and his grandfather's philosophy: "Everybody blames everybody else and they just wait for the other one to change first. We need to change first or change is not going to happen."

I no longer read Gandhi's quote as an expectation that I should change the world. Now I read it as a call for me to change. I interpret it as an admonition to transform myself.

When we experience a personal revolution, it changes the way we approach the world. We don't approach going for the incredible, sweeping significance that the world tends to celebrate. We simply hope that the way we live and the lifestyle we adopt might impact even one person for the better. That alone is significant.

On a trip to Peru, I roomed with Ben, one of our law students at Pepperdine. Ben had caught a hunger to "go and do" on a previous trip to India. One night in our tiny room, Ben shared some of his most meaningful reflections from India. He had spent a week serving in a hospital for the poor in Calcutta. As part of the experience, he spent a couple of days at Mother Teresa's mission. Ben shared how one day he washed clothes at her mission the old-fashioned way: soaking them in a giant trough and beating them on rocks to dry. Ben stepped back from his work and gasped, "Wow, look at this—this is a story I'm going to tell my grandchildren one day." In that moment, Ben realized he was part of a greater story arc. The things he was doing built a story that was a catalyst for the values he wanted to share with friends, family, and future generations. Ben's small story—washing the clothes of the sick and dying—was part of something larger that he could only barely begin to see.

It's a Lifestyle, Not a Mission

To go and do is within reach of everyone. You don't need special words to say. You don't need to be "called" or hear a supernatural voice telling you to go. I never heard one. I didn't go because of a calling, nor did I have any secret password. I just thought it would be a good experience for me. I would get a cultural education, I would learn how to volunteer my time, and it would be an adventure.

On a flight across the United States, I sat next to a man who struck up a conversation with me. He asked what I did—I was a student at the time—followed by the usual questions. *What was I studying? What did I want to do?* At that point, I wanted to work abroad as a lawyer for a particular human rights organization. The man was familiar with the organization and its work—his church donated money to the cause.

At the end of our conversation, a grin broke across the man's face. He sat back, sighed, and said, "I really hope you can go be one of those missionaries."

I cringed. Those *what*? Everything inside me ground to a halt. A *missionary*?! Did I hear that right? I wanted to be a global justice lawyer, not a missionary.

And I sat back to think. Why was I reacting so strongly? Missions work is a noble calling—so what caused my response?

The more I thought about it, the more I realized that we've created a two-camp system. If you want to go and do, you must cross from the everyone-else camp into the missionary camp. Unfortunately, this barrier keeps people like me from going because we don't feel that we fit the missionary mold. We didn't receive a call from God to the mission field. We just want to do something good and explore the world. We don't have special training or seminary degrees. We're just ordinary people who want to bring whatever skills we have to the table and show God's love through our actions—taking whatever opportunity he brings our way.

Last year at Pepperdine, a number of undergraduate seniors left for China after receiving their diplomas. They didn't go as missionaries, they went as teachers. They wanted to be present in Chinese communities, offering to teach English and help build the education system. Teaching became a vehicle for modeling Jesus' love and a platform to share the gospel—if necessary, with words. They wanted not only to bring a practical skill that would allow them to make a tangible difference in people's lives but also to use their lives as tools for spreading the message of Jesus in a closed country. These graduates saw "go and do" not as a mission, but as a lifestyle.

Katie Davis is another inspiring example. At age eighteen, she quit college and moved to Uganda, adopted thirteen children, and feeds hundreds of others. As she wrote in her book, *Kisses from Katie: A Story of Relentless Love and Redemption*, she didn't consider herself a "missionary," and though many call her one, she doesn't completely accept the branding. "Here in my home," she wrote, "I'm not a missionary or an aid worker; I am just a mom."

Saddleback Community Church is an example of an institution blurring the borders of "mission work." Under Pastor Rick Warren's leadership, Saddleback thought strategically about how it could be most effective as a church. After Warren wrote the book *The Purpose Driven Life*, he searched the globe for what might be the "purpose driven country." Rwandan President Paul Kagame stepped up and volunteered genocide-torn Rwanda as Saddleback's purpose driven country.

Saddleback soon adopted the P.E.A.C.E. Plan, a holistic transformation strategy that works to Promote reconciliation, Equip servant leaders, Assist the poor, Care for the sick, and Educate the next generation. The P.E.A.C.E. Plan might be called a mission strategy, but it's so much more than that. Saddleback adopted the country as if serving Rwanda is now a lifestyle for the church. P.E.A.C.E. teams visit regularly. On most trips, the goal is not evangelism, but working systemically to help make Rwanda a better place. Saddleback's presence on the ground is continuous. They even employ fulltime staff and facilities throughout the country.

I've participated in various missions trips over the years, the most recent a home-building trip to Mexico with my church. Although I have no construction skills, it was refreshing to build something. There's something deeply satisfying—even soulful—about creating things and working with your hands. You see results. You gain a sense of accomplishment, to the extent that it feels even more fulfilling than intellectual work.

Between lifting rafters, I thought about what a bizarre experience it must be for the family we were helping. All of a sudden, this group of Americans had come rolling into their neighborhood in nice cars, lugging cameras and power tools. It was a frenzy. The street was taken over and pretty soon word spread that we were there. Local trinket peddlers showed up to sell maracas and ponchos. By noon the next day, the house was done. From foundation to finished in little more than twenty-four hours. We didn't know the names of the people who would live there or anything about them. It was like a random act of kindness.

But is that what we really want? A lifestyle is not a series of random acts, but a strategic, long-term relationship with kindness. It's intentional. It's being willing to "go and do" whatever needs to be done whenever it needs to be done. I want the lifestyle.

Adopting a lifestyle isn't easy. It requires us to change the way we live our lives. When I left Thailand, it would have been easy to walk away. I had the badges of honor to display: photos with the kids; drawings; and, of course, stories to tell. But that wasn't enough. It was difficult to make myself call in the middle of the night when it was daytime in Thailand or to pack up Christmas presents to send. It took intentional discipline to write letters, send sponsorship money regularly, and continue studying Thai so that I could say just a few more words the next time I went. It was hard to find the time to go back again and again.

I Am

I caught wind of an undergraduate adjunct instructor at Pepperdine with a unique perspective on life. Students loved him and talked about wanting to register for his class. I walked into a session of one of his classes and took a seat. *Okay now,*

I asked myself, *who's the professor?* The room was full of college students. In the front stood a guy with long dark hair that looked like it had not seen a comb in years. He wore a plain knit beanie, jeans, and a gray Pepperdine T-shirt. Boxes of pizzas sat on the table next to him, and he talked to a group of students in big, animated gestures. I decided he couldn't be the professor—he probably delivered the pizzas. Or maybe he was some kind of technician here to help with the audiovisual stuff. He could be an old surfer who decided to go to college late in life, or a homeless guy who wandered in the door. The students surrounding him sat down, and the guy with the crazy hair and casual dress began class. That's when I met Tom Shadyac.

Tom has made some of the highest-grossing comedies of all time as a Hollywood director. His list includes hits such as *Ace Ventura: Pet Detective, The Nutty Professor, Liar Liar, Patch Adams, Bruce Almighty,* and *Evan Almighty.* Tom's class supposedly focused on screenwriting—he definitely taught what he had learned in Hollywood—but it had almost nothing to do with screenwriting. Tom's class was about life. After that class, I liked what Tom had to say so much that I sneaked in every week.

Tom had learned lessons in Hollywood about having incredible wealth and power—both of which he achieved. He stood on the very top of the mountain—a very hard to reach peak in a cutthroat industry. Tom told the class how he had it all: he owned multiple mansions in beautiful locations, went to A-list parties, and flew private jets everywhere. Despite all this, one day he stood in the foyer of one of his mansions in California. He looked around and, in a moment markedly similar to my moment in the auditorium, he realized that none of it made him happy. Tom had a personal revolution.

From that point forward, Tom began stripping off the things that didn't add to his happiness and focused on the things that did make him happy. He found that almost everything fell away. He sold the mansions and moved into a trailer. Now he flies commercial only. Instead of going to A-list parties, he goes to Africa to build orphanages and to India to help free slaves.

Through Tom's personal revolution, he found there was more to life than wealth and power. Tom's class was about passing this on to us. He didn't teach at Pepperdine for the money, he taught to start a revolution. He wanted to influence students to build a movement that adopted his lifestyle of stripping away the unnecessary to go and do the things that truly matter.

Tom didn't just talk, Tom roared with his life. He found incredible joy in giving. Tom gives away almost everything he makes now because he lives a life of service. He doesn't know whether he will direct another major film, but if he does, he will probably make millions from it. Yet the movie will be nothing more than a tool that allows him to give away more.

After finishing his major motion pictures, Tom made a documentary about his personal revolution, including the things he discovered. Tom's film *I Am* ends with a famous story about G. K. Chesterton. The British newspaper *The Times* once invited select authors to submit essays on the theme, "What's wrong with the world?" English writer and "prince of paradox," G. K. Chesterton responded with a brief letter:

"Dear Sirs, I am. Sincerely yours, G. K. Chesterton"

Tom drew the same conclusion from his personal revolution. His personal motto and the purpose of his class became "Change the world by changing ourselves." The students resonated with it, and I believe Gandhi would be proud.

Things I Need to Change

On a drive back from visiting Faifah in Burma, Faa pondered out loud, "I wonder how my life might have been different?"

At the core she was asking, "Why was I blessed and not Faifah?" Faifah's situation—disowned, deported, abused, and trafficked—is common among the hill tribal groups. Both Faa and Faifah come from the same indigenous hill tribe—the Akha people. Their parents even lived in the same village after they migrated from China. Both grew up facing the same discrimination of being the lowest hill tribe class—often considered animals. Ultimately, only subtle variations led to the great differences in their lives years later.

There were moments and interventions in Faa's life that redirected her course and kept her out of harm's way. Her life was further redirected when a friend intervened to help Faa escape her abusive household and seek refuge in a Christian home for children.

After leaving her home, Faa realized that there might be a purpose for her life—a reason that she overcame vulnerability, the struggles of hill-tribe life, and daily discrimination. Faa caught a glimpse of this reason many years later when she saw that young Akha child eating out of the trash on the street in a red-light district. In that child, I think she saw what she could have become.

That chance encounter with the child led to Faa's personal commitment to vulnerable children: to rescue them from being abused, just as she had been rescued.

Faa also stood on the mountaintop at various points. With her talent and intelligence—and being one of the few in her hill tribe who went to college—doors opened for her to leave Thailand to study and work abroad. She'd probably be a shoo-in at many graduate programs in the United States, notwithstanding countless job opportunities in Thailand. She speaks fluent English, Thai, and several hill-tribe languages—many organizations wanted her.

When I first met Faa, she was earning a sizeable income for someone her age. Yet, she felt that her heart was with the kids on the street. So Faa gave up her secure income to help build a drop-in center to encourage hill-tribe kids to stay in school and out of the red-light district. Her friends told her she was crazy because the money was too good to give up, but she pursued what made her come alive.

A couple of years later, she followed a long-held desire to study English in the United States. Yet she quickly realized that her purpose was something much larger, something she was well positioned to do—and maybe the only one who could do it.

Faa's heart to "go and do" brought her back to Thailand to start her own children's home and rescue children who were vulnerable. Still in her twenties, Faa took four, then six, then more and more children into her home. She would receive a phone call from someone who knew a child at risk. Receiving the call, Faa would travel deep into the jungle to find the village and bring the child to safety. Faa became more mother than nonprofit leader, missionary, or any other conventional title with which she might be labeled. With a house already full of kids, Faa began building her organization brick by brick, or in this case, child by child.

Faa had spent almost ten years praying for an opportunity to partner with someone or some organization that would come alongside her and allow her to pursue the call of God in her life. She had come to the US a couple of times already, but no one took her seriously when she talked about her dream. Organizations to support people like Faa have to be created.

G.R.O.W.—Grace Refuge Outreach Worldwide—is her vision for a large complex of dorms in schools in the Thai countryside, a haven for vulnerable children of all ages. Her commitment is now indefinite—she can't simply resign, leave, or take another job. Faa's personal revolution brought her to a full commitment. Now she's a living example of what that means.

"There are things I need to change," Faa told me after considering how her life might have been different.

But she wasn't setting out to change the world; rather she was trying to change herself and, in turn, the lives of a few children whose futures would be radically different if she were not there.

CHAPTER 5

Coming Alive

HALFWAY THROUGH MY FIRST TRIP to Thailand—I vividly experienced a moment of intense clarity and joy. It was on one of Thailand's sweltering, humid days, and I bicycled back to my small apartment to prepare for an evening of outreach with the kids. I was struck by the feeling that I was completely and unwaveringly happy. I had little, and I wanted nothing more. For possibly the first time in my life, I felt as though I truly wanted nothing. I was happy to simply be riding my bike and serving those in deep need.

I no longer felt trapped. It was as if I'd crawled up out of a cave and into the light aboveground. The world felt fresh. But I didn't regret the time and energy I had spent trapped. I felt as if there was a purpose for my desert—I had wandered there for a reason. Could it be that my paper and textbook prison actually started to feel worth it? It now seemed to be a small part of the journey I needed to take, a journey that humbled me and reshaped my priorities. This trip pointed me toward people like Faa, who demonstrated a "go and do" lifestyle. It pointed me toward people such as Song and Faifah who needed to be rescued as much as I did.

As best as I can describe it, I was coming alive.

Theologian Howard Thurman once wrote, "Don't ask yourself what the world needs, ask yourself what makes you come alive because the world needs people that come alive."[1]

When we come alive, we discover joy—true, constant joy. It was that moment, riding my bike in Thailand, when I felt completely and uncompromisingly happy. It was the hour playing soccer in Haiti when we all felt free and equally human. It was the visit to the school in Peru we helped fund, and the pleasure we saw on the children's faces. These joyous moments were better than any fleeting feeling of pleasure. Joy is defined as the emotion of great delight or happiness. Yet it's something so much greater, so much more sustained, and still so indescribable. We must discover and experience joy for ourselves. We know when the divine spark ignites.

What makes you come alive will be different from what makes me come alive—after all, we live in the age of personal customization. We want everything tailored to us. Our TV shows celebrate custom motorcycles, custom cars, and custom houses—everything we own must match the personality of the owner.

It's not a bad thing that we expect something unique. But in these expectations we will find ourselves drawn to specific projects and specific people that resonate with us. Our narratives will be individual narratives. There are few remaining metanarratives, few blanket solutions, few universal ideas, and few ubiquitous causes. I come alive with the things that I dream about, the stuff that keeps my mind occupied at night. These are my stories, and no one can take them away from me.

When I think about people I've seen come alive, I think about students like Brady the Revolutionary. He found something that made him come alive one semester while researching the Armenian genocide. Brady organized students to do a letter writing campaign for legislation brought before Congress. He wrote his senior thesis on the subject. He researched the issue to the extent that I wondered whether he was working on a paper or trying to fulfill some higher calling. I think he found joy in the subject—a subject that made him come alive.

The Joy of Others

There's a famous street in Santa Monica, California, where performers come every day. A group of break-dancers are there nearly every day in the same spot. They seem to love what they do—performing with passion and enthusiasm. Rightfully so as their performances attract the largest crowds once they begin. There are moves such as the windmill, where the break-dancer spins around on his shoulders, with his legs whirling above him, that really get the crowd going. I'll admit, I wouldn't normally consider break dancing, but every time I watch the dancers, I secretly wish I had that talent.

If you struggle to find the things that make you come alive, watch the joy of others. Seeing others truly happy can be enchanting. It's as if they've solved their personal revolutions and have broken through. They figured out what brings them joy and they're running after it. When we see that, we want to join in.

Every fall, I look forward to speaking to incoming law students and sharing the many opportunities to "go and do." I love

seeing the sparkle in students' eyes when they start to understand what I'm talking about. As they listen to my stories from
the field, I can tell that they are picturing themselves living out
those stories as well. These students want the same experience.
They begin to see that they, too, might have been born into a
unique set of circumstances with undeserved opportunities that
can be put to meaningful use in the world. They want to share
in the joy I've found. I know that something inside them has
started to come alive. Then when asked, "Who will go?" they
respond instantly, "I'm here, send me!"

Even more than speaking to students, I look forward to
seeing them return from their "go and do" summers. Most of
them come alive when they go and do—often for the first time.
Many discover vignettes of their purpose, part of the reason
they forged ahead for more education, and what they are ultimately working toward. They experience the raw edges of life
and want to return to those edges again.

The best part of my job is that I get to watch this. Coming
alive is the reason I took my job in the first place instead of
going to a law firm—I found something that made me come
alive and I wanted more of it. I knew more students would
come alive at Pepperdine, just like I did, if I could help show
them the way. At Pepperdine, it's been more than a program—
it's been a movement.

I'm captivated by TED Talks—short presentations by
remarkable people about "ideas worth spreading." One particular TED Talk by Derek Sivers curiously illustrated how movements form. Sivers analyzed a short video clip of an outdoor rock
concert where one person stepped into an open stretch of field
and began dancing wildly. Watching the clip, I felt embarrassed
for this idiosyncratic character. Then, after this oddball danced
alone for a while, a second person—a follower—walked up to

join and began dancing mere feet away. A few seconds later, a third joined, then a fourth, then a fifth. Within seconds, hordes of people flooded in from all over the concert grounds to join what became a giant dance party.

The key to starting a movement, Sivers suggested, is not the first person, but the second—the follower. The follower legitimizes the first and convinces the crowd that the activity is worthwhile. Movements don't start with one person; they start with two or more.

When we see joy in others, we need to step out and join them. We might get to share in their joy, or it might serve as a guidepost to our own unique purpose. But we can also play a larger role. We can help build movements. When we follow, we validate valuable people and we validate the joy of others. We get to help fulfill American anthropologist Margaret Mead's famous quote: "A small group of thoughtful people could change the world. Indeed, it's the only thing that ever has."[2]

Of the things I enjoy most in life, few were discovered of my own volition. It was always someone else's incurable enthusiasm that pointed me in that direction. When we find something that makes us come alive, we want to share in that joy.

Encountering God

When I talk about joy, I'm talking about true joy—not just the pursuit of happiness. I've experienced things that I thought would bring me great joy, but they only let me down as a mere fleeting pleasure. I think about vehicles that I have owned or wanted to own. They seemed like status symbols and a place to rest my identity, but in the end, they turned out to be mere vehicles that lost their luster. I think about sports I've competed in where I was happy only when I was winning. While the pleasure of victory was intense, it quickly faded away. I fear that high paying jobs could end the same way—I'd be tempted with fleeting pleasures instead of being fulfilled by joy.

On one trip to Thailand, I stumbled upon the entrance to a prayer labyrinth. Spread before me as a fifty-foot-diameter circle, the labyrinth was composed of low-lying shrubs, a precise maze cut into the greenery that revealed a gravel footpath. The maze twisted and turned, filling the whole circle, until its end at a prominent rock in the center. The objective of the labyrinth involved arriving at the rock.

Adopted by the Christian church in medieval times, labyrinths symbolize the journey to God. Each labyrinth represents the proprietor's personal journey, the twists and turns in the path reflect the twists and turns in life. Walking the path constitutes an act of worship, with each step a prayer from the entire body.

If we determine what's important to God, we uncover a road map through our labyrinth. Even though we must still endure all the twists and turns, we can anticipate the next bend and move through the labyrinth of life with increasing tempo. When we have our bearings, we have direction, with the things important to God as a beacon to guide us.

Joy is one of those beacons. We know that God loves joy. As the psalmist tells us, "You will show me the way of life, granting me the joy of your presence and the pleasures of living with you forever." There's some kind of important connection between joy, the things in which God takes pleasure, and our paths in life. When I reflect on experiencing joy as I "go and do," I feel as though in those moments I have entered the presence of God.

"Nothing is as dangerous as encountering the true and living God," writes Mark Labberton in his book *The Dangerous Act of Worship*. "Why? Because meeting God redefines everything we call normal and commands us to seek first his kingdom (Matthew 6:33)."[3]

In the presence of those street kids in Thailand, I felt as if I was in the presence of God, the dangerous, true, and living God. For me, it wasn't dangerous in the way you might expect—it wasn't the risky trips into Burma or the precarious work in the red-light district. Encountering God meant that I was faced with the choice of whether I wanted to build his Kingdom or mine. And I was either in or out.

This encounter is, indeed, dangerous. It's dangerous because we often stumble upon God in the places we least expect, and often don't want to enter. It's dangerous because it draws us back again and again. I know because I found God in a red-light district full of street kids. I didn't want to. I fought it. But in the end, the authentic encounter drew me back again and again.

Whether we realize it or not, our desire to "go and do" is a desire to meet God—sometimes for the first time.

In 2009, Gary Haugen, president and CEO of the International Justice Mission, delivered the commencement speech at Pepperdine's School of Law. Haugen spoke about joy. Addressing a group of soon-to-be lawyers, he noted that many lawyers don't experience true and lasting joy. There may be moments of excitement and pleasure, but these are often fleeting. Joylessness can plague any profession and rob it of the ability to come alive. But this doesn't have to be the case.

Haugen echoed the experiences of those who "go and do." He knows firsthand, as a lawyer who founded a leading "go and do" organization. At the crux of Haugen's speech he told the audience, "I found the easy way to make your life in the law matter is to simply have it connect to the world of desperate human need, and I mean desperate human need. To run to the places in our world where literally people die if the lawyers don't show up."[4]

He continued with statistics that describe the deplorable condition of our world: More than 27 million individuals held in slavery. Countries existing in which 40 percent of girls under fourteen are victims of rape or attempted rape. Sixty to 85 percent of prisoners in the developing world have never been convicted or even charged with a crime. His message was clear: the world is hurting.

Haugen continued, "This then is the great paradox facing the legal profession in your age. On the one hand we have a vast, empowered, and well-resourced legal profession in the West that is threatened with joylessness and ennui because of its alienation from the heroic. On the other hand, we have the vast world of the global poor whose most fundamental problem is lawlessness. . . . I believe there is in this generation a vast mutual rescue just waiting to happen. A rescue of the poor from relentless oppression and a rescue of the legal profession from a joyless disconnect from heroic purpose."

"A vast mutual rescue": I can feel it—I've been a participant. But, it's not only the legal profession; it's in each of us in every profession and place in life. I see this need crying out in my peers, so many like me who are crying out to be rescued from careers and lives disconnected from a heroic purpose. We just want to be connected to something that matters. And there are so many on the other side, waiting to be rescued, desperate to know they matter.

God's Great Exchange Program

There are, indeed, places in our world where people literally die if doctors don't show up, if social workers don't show up, if people of any stripe don't show up to simply hand out food, blankets, clean water, or vaccinations. Our need for purpose matches someone's need for survival. "Go and do" rescues us as we rescue others—it's like God's great exchange program. We are standing on the precipice of this vast mutual rescue where we can choose now how we want to live the rest of our lives. We can make it our lifestyle and vocation.

As author Frederick Buechner wrote, "Vocation is where our deep gladness meets the world's deep need."[5] God's great exchange points us toward our vocation. The irony of the exchange is that as we seek to rescue those in deep need, it's often we ourselves who equally need to be rescued.

When my nose was buried in my law textbooks, I desperately needed to be rescued. Thankfully, I dared myself to throw my hat in the ring of God's great exchange. I discovered purpose in the lives of those I could help rescue. I experienced joy as I found myself close to desperate human suffering. I found deep gladness close to the kids in Thailand because I stepped into the presence of God. When the street kids rescued me, I unearthed a tiny point where my deep gladness met a great need, and in turn, I discovered my vocation.

I'm reminded of a scene from the movie *Fight Club*.

Brad Pitt plays Tyler Durden, the charismatic alter ego of the unnamed "everyman" narrator. He's a depressed office worker looking to escape his meaningless life. In the nighttime scene, Durden walks by a convenience store, spontaneously runs inside, pulls the store clerk out to the curb, and puts a gun to his head.

"What did you want to be?" Tyler Durden asks the hysterical convenience store clerk as he cocks his gun.

After a while, the clerk finally mumbles, "A veterinarian."

Durden asks for the clerk's wallet and opens it. The clerk's name: Raymond K. Hessel. Along with his ID, Durden finds an expired community college card. Did you ever finish your degree? Durden asks. Hessel shakes his head—no. Durden decides to keep the ID card listing Hessel's address, telling him that he will check up on him in a few months. If Hessel's not on his way to being a veterinarian, he will be dead.

After Hessel disappears into the night, Tyler Durden looks up with satisfaction and says, "Tomorrow will be the most beautiful day of Raymond K. Hessel's life. His breakfast will taste better than any meal you and I have ever tasted."

Fight Club is not about fighting at all. Quite the contrary, it's about living. It's about living out who we truly want to be.

I like the scene because the clerk had given up on his dreams, surrendering who he wanted to be. Unfortunately, to go and live those dreams, he had to be taken to the edge of his life, with a gun to his head. And when you think about it, that bit of fiction isn't so far from reality—is it?

I don't want to get to a point where my dreams have become so far removed from me that I need to stare death in the face in order to start living them, do you? I want to continue to discover the things that make me come alive and chase after them daily.

When you come alive, every day is the most beautiful day and every breakfast is the best meal you have ever tasted. You struggle to fall asleep because you'd rather keep going. You wake up before your alarm clock goes off because you can't wait to get back at it. You know what you're doing has purpose. It matters. You matter.

CHAPTER 6

We Are the Solution

GONE. The power cut out again, cloaking our chairs in a sudden veil of black and silencing our conversation—nothing unexpected, though. The power supply regularly shifted between cities in Bangladesh for lack of a sufficient electrical grid. This was our hour of darkness in Salanga, a tiny village barely on the map located in northern Bangladesh. But it was fine—the lack of electricity provided a reason to sit on the roof and soak in the meager breeze. The relentless heat and humidity made us so exhausted that no muscle wanted to move. With no clocks, I lost track of time but guessed it to be after ten p.m. Two hours earlier, seeking a moment of relief, I had poured a bucket of cool water on my head, and my clothes still felt damp. Bangladesh in the summer proved to be one of the hottest, most humid experiences of my life. Hours after an evening game of soccer with local kids, I was still sweating. The bucket of water had done little to cool me.

My simple dare to travel to Thailand for my "go and do" summer had brought me much farther than expected—an opportunity arose for field research in Bangladesh with Grameen Bank. Along with its founder, Dr. Muhammad Yunus, Grameen Bank had won the Nobel Peace Prize that spring for developing the practice of microfinance—the process of giving small loans to the very poor. I went to Bangladesh to learn about the mechanics of microfinance and assess its impact.

At any point earlier in my life, if I had sat down to map out a list of the countries I hoped to visit or thought I would ever visit, Bangladesh would have been one of the last. I never expected to set foot there. If someone had told me, even a year ago, that Bangladesh might be a place that would help fuel my desire to "go," I would have laughed nervously and explained that they had notified the wrong person. It's funny how places you never expect to end up and people you never expect to meet can suddenly spring up on you in remarkable ways. Like the flip of a light switch, you find a whole new part of yourself illuminated.

Suddenly, the lights flickered back on. Our band of American travelers atop the roof let out a collective groan. The bright light emanating from the nearby doorway blinded me, piercing the peacefulness of the evening and reminding me that I must eventually crawl into a hot, stuffy bed.

"Come downstairs," our translator beckoned from the stairwell, silhouetted in the brightly lit doorway.

"No thanks," we all replied, feeling content in our stillness.

"Please, come downstairs," he insisted. "The bank manager wants to talk to you." Sensing urgency in his voice, we reluctantly started moving to depart our rooftop relief. Was there a problem?

We trudged downstairs and stumbled into the bank office. This rural branch of Grameen Bank, the microfinance provider, appeared pastoral—a two-story brick building in the middle of endless rice fields—and particularly plain on the inside. Much to our surprise, the bank manager and nine regional managers surrounded a large table, seated in anticipation of our arrival.

"What questions do you have for them?" our translator asked us as the managers pulled chairs up to the table. We glanced at one another with knowing looks: did we have questions? We eventually surmised an expectation in Bangladesh that we must ask questions—whether or not we actually had them.

After improvising a few questions about Grameen Bank's structure and its customers, I turned the tables: "Do you have any questions for us?" Unlike my compatriots and me, the bank staff came armed and loaded—as if waiting for this moment for years. Their questions quickly turned to American politics and foreign policy, to which they appeared more in tune than many Americans I know. These rural Bengali bankers wanted our opinions and insights, treating every word as if it were an official statement from the United States government.

Demonstrating their awareness of American current events, these bankers proceeded to tell us which candidate would win the upcoming American election. Despite our explanation that the president was chosen through a working democratic voting process and that we did not yet know who the winning candidate would be, our audience protested, insisting that they knew, unwaveringly, who would become president.

Although Bangladesh officially calls itself a democracy, the power shifts primarily between two families. As described to me, the winning family is the one who hands out the greatest number of free cigarettes—one cigarette buys one vote.

Questions turned from politics to our life in America. What

did we do? What kind of houses did we have? Were we married? And the conversation eventually ventured into faith. The bankers with us in the room were all devout Muslims, and many had likely not encountered a Christian before that night.

As one of our English answers was being translated, I realized that we were ambassadors for our country and our faith. The three of us were likely the first Americans and Christians they had ever met and maybe the only ones they would ever meet. I felt strange, knowing that we were responsible for representing 300 million Americans and 2.1 billion Christians.

My unexpected sensation of being an ambassador continued after I retired to my room for the evening. I reflected on my entire time in Bangladesh and started to see the role of my team as more than observation and research. We may not have had an official political appointment, but the three of us were truly ambassadors.

Our ambassadorial status extended beyond the confines of the bank walls. We were ambassadors through our actions in the village, our visits to farmers out in the rice paddies, and our evenings playing soccer with the local kids. The most exciting news in town that week was that three Americans roamed the streets. News spread quickly. Throngs of people would gather to watch us. They waved as we coasted by on rickshaws, and children ran alongside us. Those who owned cameras photographed us incessantly. Our rickshaws felt like a motorcade, and we were the celebrities. I would be surprised if many other Westerners had ever visited this remote village, or ever would. Every move we made was noticed. Every step we took left an impression and formed their judgment of Americans and Christians. What kind of example did we leave? Did we leave a better impression of our country? More importantly, did our example rise to meet the standards of our faith?

People Skills

I used to envy doctors. They could show up anywhere and provide a useful skill. Whenever I visit rural villages or urban slums or anyplace with limited medical access, undoubtedly people with a treatable medical problem come forward to ask for help. They usually cannot afford treatment, so they suffer quietly. I always wish I could help.

If you're like me, you don't have a readily applicable skill like doctors do. Or, at least, we think we don't because we don't possess a special certification or license. I learned, to my surprise, that we have much to offer as we "go" out into the world, even as ordinary citizens.

We are ambassadors. We don't need political appointments. We are instantly appointed merely by "go-ing." We serve as ambassadors for our faith, our countries, our communities, our nonprofits, our schools. We need to recognize and embrace this opportunity whether we like it or not. We should learn to like it. And more, we should learn to leverage it.

More than ever, we must become private ambassadors. The world is changing. Nation-states are fracturing and becoming diluted, quickly making them less powerful. Growing distrust abounds in the ability of governments to solve global problems.

Multinational organizations are becoming even more ineffective. For example, the operations and achievements of the United Nations confound most people. Those nations who are in the UN, including the United States, seem to have dwindling faith in the organization as it now stands. According to its charter in 1945, the UN intended to resolve external conflicts between countries. Today, most of the UN's work attempts to resolve internal conflicts within countries—namely peacekeeping and development. The world has changed, and the demands of governments and multinational organizations have outgrown their original purposes.

Trust now shifts from governments and multinationals to people. Yes, people. Private citizens. People—individuals, small organizations, and churches—must take matters into their own hands.

Consider some recent diplomatic events. The US government did not arrange for the release of political prisoners from North Korea. Jimmy Carter and Bill Clinton went independently on separate diplomatic missions to bring back Americans locked up in the small, isolated nation. Previous service as US presidents made them naturally compelling figures, but it was private individuals, not governments, that won the day. Private individuals—unofficial diplomats—made these recoveries happen. The United States remains in a stalemate with the North Koreans, further illustrating that governments lose the agility to problem solve amid the heavy balancing of foreign policy.

Other private citizens have recognized this growing need. Carne Ross is a private citizen taking matters into his own hands. He served as a British diplomat before becoming disenchanted with his country's foreign policy and its response to a changing world. Ross founded an organization he named "Independent Diplomat" where he does exactly that—he independently represents those who lack a voice on the world stage. For example, he serves as an independent diplomat for leaders in southern Sudan trying to form a new nation and for the ethnic groups in Burma who want to be recognized as official political parties, just to name a few.

Ross points out that, in recent years, nation states began fracturing and becoming less powerful. "The game has changed," as he puts it. Governments aren't set up to solve the complex problems facing the world, so they won't be the solution. He believes in people—private citizens, he says, will be the solution.[6]

An Ambassadorial Appointment

March 20, 2003, came only days after my twenty-first birthday. I recall staying up late that night in my dorm—late enough that almost all the freshmen had gone to bed. I sat in the common area watching TV, glued to CNN. That night, coalition forces had begun the incursion into the Basra province in Iraq.

"Shock and Awe" had happened the night before, and news analysts were predicting an easy, potentially bloodless sweep of Iraq. News crews broadcast images of people in Basra celebrating the invasion, tearing down posters of Saddam Hussein and welcoming US troops.

A large portion of my generation went through high school and college watching our country fight two wars. The wars, unfortunately, were not as quick or easy as was hoped. They took their toll on our country and even divided us. In 2008, the year I graduated law school, the economy went berserk and the job market collapsed. These events sit fresh in the minds of all of us, coloring our view of the world.

As I wrote this, various influential voices called for US intervention in the Congo to stop the Lord's Resistance Army rebel group or to enter Burma to take down the junta or to attack Iran by striking weapons sites or to respond to North Korea's nuclear threats. A definite time and place exist for government intervention, but those instances appear to be decreasing. We seek to interact and influence our government, but we know that government presents an unlikely solution.

Governments can do only so much. They must deal with complicated foreign policy issues like a vastly complex game of chess. Closer to home, the financial crisis finds the national government as well as local governments dramatically cutting back budgets to stay afloat. For those who are ready to be "doing," waiting on the government is not good enough when people are dying of preventable problems.

Where do we turn? We turn to each other. It's up to us—each one of us. There is no one else. There is no backup plan. We have no choice but to go out when we see a problem, because we know that no one else may respond. These issues are, indeed, our problems. Martin Luther King Jr. once wrote, "Injustice anywhere is a threat to justice everywhere."[7] The same can be said for humanity. Any threat to human dignity is a threat to us personally. If we are to simply stand by, then what good are we?

But there's even more to it than that.

The apostle Paul deputizes us—the community of believers—as ambassadors. Twice Paul called himself an ambassador and then said that we are all ambassadors for Christ. In 2 Corinthians 5:19-21, Paul writes,

> God was in Christ, reconciling the world to himself,
> no longer counting people's sins against them. And
> he gave us this wonderful message of reconciliation.
> So we are Christ's ambassadors; God is making his
> appeal through us. We speak for Christ when we plead,
> "Come back to God!" For God made Christ, who
> never sinned, to be the offering for our sin, so that we
> could be made right with God through Christ.

I think it's significant that here Paul doesn't ask us to be preachers or evangelists, but to be ambassadors. This deputation offers much to unpack and casts a wide net for the ambassadorial appointment. It certainly delivers a call to action for us to go out and reconcile the world to God and to be reconciled with one another. If nothing else, Paul suggests that we all have the capability as private individuals to serve the world as ambassadors for the things that are important to God. I believe that includes more than looking at the spirit alone. James gives us a clue when he tells us that the religion our Father considers pure and beyond reproach is the one that looks after those who would otherwise be alone with their need (see James 1:27).

What would it mean for us to act as ambassadors of our faith? We should be engaged in the study of diplomacy. We should seek opportunities to exercise this deputation. If the church—the body of Christ—is God's plan for the world, then it's up to us. We can't expect governments to succeed after a track record of failures. It's our turn to step up to the global plate.

Citizen diplomacy will be needed more than ever in the coming years, especially for the Christian church and our faith. When I wrote this book, a debate about a mosque at Ground Zero waged in New York City while in another state a church created controversy over a threat to burn the Koran. I was traveling in Southeast Asia as this latter controversy unfolded, and it sparked various outbursts of violence—church burnings and murders in parts of rural India and Indonesia. The matter reaches beyond any single country or nation-state; it transcends borders.

Former British prime minister Tony Blair has asked: "Does religious faith become a force for progress? Or does religious faith become a source of conflict and sectarianism? I think that's the dominant question of the 21st century."[8] Religious freedom versus intolerance may be one of the greatest issues facing us in the coming years. This struggle will only continue to grow. Religions will continue to collide and, undoubtedly, we will see more episodes of anger and violence. Building bridges will require ambassadors who, like the issues, are also able to transcend borders.

Blair, who founded his Tony Blair Faith Foundation for this purpose, believes that faith can, indeed, become a force for global progress. Secular governments are in no position and have no desire to accomplish this. Without action by private citizens and organizations responding to this ambassadorial goal of progress, faith may become the great divider.

The Role of an Ambassador

I've been privileged to meet and get to know a few ambassadors and diplomats. Charged with representing a nation, ambassadors serve as the highest-ranking diplomats from their countries. For most ambassadors, reaching such a prestigious position marks the pinnacle of their careers. In the case of the United States, ambassadors handle the affairs of the country on behalf of the State Department. They are the president's hands and feet abroad.

Ambassadors don't exist to make everyone a citizen of his or her nation. Rather, they represent the interests of their sending country. They must represent something—a goal, an idea, a vision. They further the goal or idea or vision by organizing important meetings, bringing people together, assisting their citizens, networking with the highest officials in other countries, and collaborating with key institutions. Ambassadors also carry messages from their sending country—messages of friendship, messages of collaboration, and messages that embody the interests of those they represent. Oftentimes, a primary function of ambassadors is simply being present. They attend events and meetings to show their support and lend credibility—they frequently influence by action, not necessarily by words.

Ambassadors don't have typical nine-to-five jobs. They are always on duty. Those on foreign assignments often live in the host country in large houses built for entertaining. One event typically flows into the next, packing each day's schedule. Being an ambassador is a lifestyle. The diplomatic hats never come off; they are always on display.

This is the diplomacy we need to learn. We need to carry a message of faith or a vision for a better world, at all times, everywhere we go. We need to seek the opportunities to share that message. We need to bring people together, lend our credibility, and be present. We need to engage in a steady stream of diplomacy.

A Surprising Admission

A few years ago I developed an affinity for a beautiful, but dangerous, country—one of the least-developed nations on earth. For years, the country has been ruled by a brutal military regime that operates with blatant disregard for its citizens. Yet, the wonderful people drew me in and kept me going back. Because of my travels there, I developed a network of friends at home advocating freedom in that country.

At a meeting of a group of these friends, we all discussed what strategies were available to pressure the brutal dictatorship to stop its actions.

"How can we get these dictators to the United States for a dialogue?" someone posed. No one had a plausible solution.

"Well, they're already here," I interjected. "They have an embassy in Washington, DC. Has anyone been there to meet with the ambassador?" No one responded.

"What if we made an appointment with the ambassador and tried to be friends?" I suggested.

I received mostly blank stares in return. I had the audacity to suggest that we engage the enemy—as friends. This dictator's sole representative to the most powerful country on earth was already on our shores. Could we really be friends?

I visited DC a few months later, but I did not take the initiative to reach out to the embassy. On the flight home, my lack
of initiative weighed heavy on my heart. I wondered what Jesus
might have done—I thought he might attempt to sit down with
the dictator's representative and just try to be friends, similar to
the way he sat down with the tax collector. What story would
he have wanted me to tell in this situation?

I hoped for another opportunity. Six months later, another
trip to DC came up. My previously missed opportunity caught
up with me. Was this going to turn into another dare? It made
me nervous, but it kept gnawing at me. I thought to myself,
Remember how this turned out the last time you felt like this? With
a strong track record of some of the best experiences of my life,
I dared myself to follow the call.

I drafted a letter to the ambassador and faxed it to the
embassy. I waited a week: no response. I called the embassy
and spoke to the receptionist. She was surprised—she hadn't
received a fax. She gave me a different number, and I refaxed
the letter immediately. A few more days went by and still no
response. My travel date was closing in, but I was determined.

I called again and explained the situation. "Just a minute,
please let me check." She set the phone down, and a minute
later a loud rustling began.

"Hello?" came a deep male voice with a heavy accent.

"Uh, hello, my name is Jay Milbrandt, and I work for
Pepperdine University School of Law. I'm calling because I
love your country—I've visited five times—and I would really
like to meet with you. Could I visit you next week when I'm
in DC?"

"Yes, I read your letter," the voice replied, confirming that I
was, indeed, speaking with the ambassador. He sounded excited.
"The place you visited is where I'm from in the country!"

"Oh, really? It's so beautiful there!" We briefly discussed local cuisine and notable landmarks—we'd eaten in the same restaurants and walked the same streets.

"When do you want to come to the embassy?"

"Tuesday or Wednesday?" I said warily. Usually the ambassador tells you when to come.

"Okay, Tuesday or Wednesday is fine."

"Tuesday is best for me," I suggested. "Does that work for you?"

"Yes, what time will you come?"

"One or two o'clock?" I was still bewildered by the free rein on the ambassador's calendar that I'd been granted.

"Yes, one or two o'clock is fine," he replied.

"Two," I suggested, searching for something definite. He agreed.

In disbelief, I hung up the phone. That went better than I could have ever expected.

On Tuesday, at 1:59 p.m., I found the front steps to the embassy. An embassy staffer opened the door as I walked up the stairs—they were awaiting my arrival. The staffer quickly ushered me into a sitting room off the main lobby.

The ambassador entered, overflowing with excitement to meet me. Let me remind you that I am no one of importance. I don't represent a government, multinational agency, or even a corporation interested in investing. I'm simply someone who had visited his nation. We disagree on his country's domestic policy, and we have different faiths. Yet we shook hands and sat down before a tray of tea and tarts.

For the next forty-five minutes, we had one of the best, most engaging conversations I'd ever had with anyone. We talked about our jobs, the beauty of his country and its wonderful cuisine, how long he had served his nation, where his kids went to school, and what he planned to do after he retires. We spoke as if we were old friends.

I approached the conversation as a friend, as someone who cared about the people of his nation, and as someone who would be happy to collaborate with his country. I avoided anything even remotely condemning. He knew that I was not oblivious to the news and that I had witnessed the horrible things happening in his country.

Suddenly, halfway through our conversation his posture and his voice changed. "You know, our legal system is broken; there is no justice," he admitted in a hushed tone. "This is not my government's position; this is my own opinion."

Shocked, my jaw hit the floor. I had avoided politics up to this point.

"Yes, I know that many people are critical of your government," I replied. "There are likewise many things to be critical of here in the United States. No country is perfect. But I hope that the relationship between our countries will improve. I work for a university, and we don't have a political agenda. Maybe we can use this position to start building a friendship and dialogue."

He heartily agreed. "Everyone misunderstands our country," he lamented. "They don't know the whole story."

We talked longer over our tea and tarts. Out of respect for his time, I made three offers throughout our meeting to let him return to his duties, but the ambassador extended the conversation each time. Forty-five minutes after what I thought would be a five-minute meet and greet, I was finally walking toward the door.

Before I stepped back outside, the ambassador stopped me. "It's so nice to actually have someone visit who likes our country."

As I walked back to my hotel, I marveled at what had happened. The ambassador had made astounding, unanticipated admissions. But more important, we became friends. I left with his personal e-mail address and an agreement from him to visit me in California. To many of my friends, this ambassador represented the enemy. One-on-one, however, we were both people who had substantial common ground, even though we were in opposite camps. I got through to him because I was one of the only people who had not come as an enemy. I wondered why no one had tried this earlier.

An Audience with a President

One winter, I flew into a tiny African republic for a meeting. Before I arrived, through some strategic Google searching and a few well-worded e-mails, I had a tentative commitment from the president's secretary for a meeting with the president. Again, I was nobody—a kid from an American university in his late twenties—so I could easily get bumped for any reason. He'd had to bump me on a previous visit due to an important, last-minute matter. Yet I figured it was worth another try. Now, on the ground, it was a waiting game. A few calls and text messages to his office received no response—and tomorrow was supposed to be the day. Then, a late-evening message arrived from his secretary: a new meeting time, but it was definitely on. *Whew*—a sigh of relief.

The next morning, I cleared heavy security and received protocol instructions. The courtyard created a long walk from the guard booth to the presidential palace. I thought to myself, *Is this really happening?* The president's secretary escorted me to the conference center—an oversized room with fancy chairs and large oil paintings on the walls depicting African history. The chairs sat in a square without a table, the president's chair open at the head. Cabinet members and officials from his staff entered to take some of the remaining chairs. We waited for the president to enter.

Minutes later, he arrived with a trail of secretaries and photographers. He had come immediately after signing an official declaration. Introductions were formal: I called him "Your Excellency." I was nobody, but I had an audience with the president. We discussed our programs in his country, and I invited him to Pepperdine. He agreed to all requests and gave an official commitment from his government.

As I walked back across the wide courtyard, my heart raced. I asked myself aloud, "Did that really happen?" Yes. It took a moment for this notion to settle. I'd arranged a meeting with the president, the head of state for an entire nation. We sat and discussed projects for furthering the rule of law in his country, and I left with a commitment, even though I was just a private individual who represented a university in America. This had happened because I'd reached out—because I tried. It would have been much, much easier not to try.

We often don't realize how accessible important decision makers can be. Why? Because we don't try. We wrongly believe that we have nothing to offer or that they would never meet with us. And we don't have to take a fifteen-hour plane ride and brave security checks to think this way. We can do the same with local leaders, faith groups near our homes, or causes that we admire.

I'm inspired by the work of the Tony Blair Faith Foundation. It has taken a field that was once left to governments and heads of religious orders—reconciliation and bridge building—and exported it into the realm of everyday people, with an emphasis on dialogue between major religions. In universities around the world, the foundation has inserted a high level of diplomacy into the classroom and found ways to encourage common citizens to engage others in the discussion.

We can all engage as citizen diplomats. If we thought of ourselves in this light, we might be bolder and more intentional with our interactions. We might reach out to some of the highest offices and insert our own voices into the global dialogue.

We might befriend those who seemingly have few friends. We might start a conversation about difficult topics. We might work toward reconciliation between conflicting faiths or ideologies. At our core, we are all human and we all have hope in something. And that, if nothing else, is a starting point.

The Citizen Ambassador

I have friends who told me that their dream was to work for the United Nations, to represent our country, or to help broker peace. But, alas, they didn't get the right degree or their career paths took them in the wrong direction or now they've got two small kids who tie them to home. But citizen ambassador is a field that does exist, and it's accessible to everyone.

When we typically think of ambassadors, we think of a high level of official, direct, government-to-government diplomacy. A select few people have this opportunity. Most of us will never work for the US State Department or in the Foreign Service. But that doesn't leave us out.

For the rest of us without political appointments, we have citizen diplomacy. If you need a technical name to legitimize this field of study and practice, it's known as "track II diplomacy." This track II diplomacy engages regular people—such as members of the business community, religious clergy, or even you and me—in the global dialogue. This dialogue seeks to influence society at its highest levels. When we "go" on behalf of an institution, a school, a church, or an idea, we are working as citizen ambassadors.

Then there's a third level that some like to call track III diplomacy—a fancy term for what most of us already unknowingly practice each day. Through the work of regular people, communities of faith, schools, and nonprofits, we create a dialogue with our counterparts locally and around the world. This track III diplomacy often involves organizing conferences, advocacy, media campaigns, and conversations.

How does this play out? For instance, there's a group at Pepperdine that goes to the Middle East to engage various adversarial religious groups in healthy dialogue. Or, there's my meeting in Bangladesh where I was an ambassador to the bankers. Locally, this summer I brought together the Karen refugees from Burma to share their stories with the city and church communities where they've settled. And at Pepperdine we continually bring members of Christianity, Islam, and Judaism together in an effort to find common ground.

What does this mean for us? We do not realize the power we can wield just as we are. Through friendships and diplomacy, we can influence governments, resolve conflicts, offer assistance, and represent those who have no voice. We don't have to wait for an official summons or a conflict to resolve. We're not required to possess a particular degree or specialized training. We go to build friendships and confidence. We can tell our counterparts how much we love their countries or neighborhoods. We can tell them how much we like their people or that their food is fantastic or what we respect about their faith. Or we can simply ask how old their kids are and what they like to do with their free time. If we work at it, we can build bridges, bring those in need of a voice into the conversation, and influence the course of humanity.

Recognizing that we are participating in a legitimate field of action is a helpful starting point. Knowing that our conversation is more than mere conversation gives us the courage to take the initiative and put in place events that bring people together. And at a minimum, our posture changes and our professionalism soars when we know that we are playing an important role as citizen ambassadors.

A few years ago, I heard that the small city of Midland, Texas, had shifted the tide in Sudan. Could that be true? With fewer than one hundred thousand people in the flatlands of Texas, Midland doesn't come to mind when I think of world affairs. But its ambitious "go and do" spirit led its citizenry to take a "behind-the-scenes role in the Sudanese peace talks, conducting diplomacy directly with the government of Sudan."[9]

According to the *American Spectator*:

In March 2003, Midlanders city-wide—from Methodist to Baptist ministers, from the Mayor and city councilmen to oil company executives and housewives, from the Catholic bishop to Lutheran and Episcopalian pastors—sent a letter to the government of Sudan, calling for a just peace in the 20-year war between Christians and Muslims.

"Ministerial Alliance of Midland, Texas," read the letterhead. "Hometown of President Bush and First Lady Laura Bush." The letter's underlying message to Khartoum: work towards a just peace or Bush's hometown will put pressure on the U.S. government to enforce the Sudan Peace Act, legislation passed in 2002 which requires that the White House monitor negotiations between the Sudanese government and the rebels in the Sudan People's Liberation Army.

The Midlanders' letter got the attention of Khartoum. Khidir H. Ahmed, the Sudanese ambassador to the United States, told me that Sudan's Minister of Foreign Affairs Mustafa Osman Ismail encouraged him to talk with the Christians from the "village of George Bush" and invite them to visit Khartoum. "We have been talking since that time," says Ahmed.[10]

The Midland group communicated directly with the Sudanese government, rebel groups, the US State Department, and churches in Sudan to help steer the peace talks. Led by individuals who describe themselves as "housewives" and "ranchers' daughters," the Midland model shows what can be possible.

This might be the fringes of a new field of collective action. Diplomacy is an art. Diplomacy is also a lifestyle. It's something we need to study and something we need to practice. Particularly for the church today—with witness for our God so often lacking—this idea of diplomacy ministry might be one of the next frontiers. It's more action than words. Oftentimes it is simply being present—lending our support and affirmation to the things we believe are important.

For me, my time spent in Bangladesh and Thailand empowered me to be an ambassador for those whose voices needed a megaphone. My trip to Bangladesh turned into a short documentary film on the effect of microfinance—I profiled the lives I saw changed. The film was selected for an international film festival, touring sixteen countries and eighteen venues from the United States to Australia to Liberia. For my kids in Thailand, their statelessness turned into a published academic article proposing a solution to the crisis as well as another short documentary on statelessness in general. And on behalf of the people of Burma, I've been asked to dialogue with government officials about their plight, speak at churches, and organize conferences on the subject. Throughout all this, I simply took what I learned and positioned myself as an informal ambassador. My reach extended further than I could have ever imagined.

One of my trips to Uganda coincided with the annual opening day of the Ugandan court system. Opening day consists of fanfare as the judiciary renews its call to do justice in Uganda. Pomp and circumstance abound on the front lawn of Uganda's iconic, British-colonial era, High Court building. A giant tent where the judiciary sits faces a crowd of hundreds. The judges don their flowing robes and traditional white wigs. Dancers twirl to the pulsating rhythm of ethnic drums. All the lawyers show up, and even the press clamors for photo ops. It felt like a mix of college graduation and a presidential inauguration.

I was with a small team of three from our university. Our friends in the Ugandan judiciary invited us to the event. When we arrived, it had already begun and a woman who appeared to be expecting us ushered us into the main tent. She seated us in a row with a sign marked "Ambassadors." We faced the crowd, with the judges seated in the row immediately in front of us. Seated next to us were the actual ambassadors from various nations. They were simply present. No speeches, no meetings. The ambassadors' presence demonstrated their support for the judiciary and the importance of the rule of law.

I whispered to my colleagues that we must be considered at the level of ambassadors. We all grinned and chuckled, enjoying a fleeting moment of feigned significance. But, as I reflected later, it wasn't that far from the truth. We *were* ambassadors.

Much like in Bangladesh, we were there to represent not only our school but also our country and our faith. Our message was justice and friendship. Our presence showed that we supported the leaders of this country—that across the ocean they had friends who supported and admired what they did. We were simply present. And that was diplomacy.

When we start seeing ourselves as "citizen ambassadors," the sky is the limit for where our ambassadorship could take us. We might end up building better schools in our communities or creating peace in foreign countries. We may find ourselves becoming local leaders for a cause or advocating for children an ocean away. We may even find ourselves eventually invited to sit with ambassadors and presidents. While we might not see our trajectory at first, it always starts with a few intentional first steps.

That first step is seeing ourselves as ambassadors for some important purpose.

CHAPTER 7

Bold Explorations

I WAS IN PAIN. It was cold, the coldest part of night—just before morning. I could barely take another step. The air felt so thin that every breath took effort. Every couple of steps, I stopped to gasp for air. I couldn't feel my toes. The heat packs in my mountaineering boots seemed to make no difference. I reached for the tube on my hydration pack and found that the entire thing, even the bladder of water deep in my backpack, was completely frozen.

I started to feel lightheaded. My balance faded. The small glow of my headlamp appeared to shrink—or was the world closing in around me? "I think I'm going to pass out," I said with slurred speech. Godlisten, my guide, grabbed my arm and sat me down. I reclined on the cold rocks, trying to pull myself together.

Godlisten broke into praise songs as we rested—his joy lifted our spirits. Walking all day, we had asked him endless questions about his life. As a teenager, Godlisten had started portering for climbers on Mount Kilimanjaro. It was a hard job to land, and he worked his way up the ranks after years of portering—up to assistant guide, then finally a full guide. Godlisten must have climbed Kilimanjaro hundreds of times—going nearly every other week. He demonstrated servant leadership, patiently guiding every step while making sure the magic happened behind the scenes without our knowing it. Yet, I could tell the mountain had taken its toll on him—the accumulation of climbing injuries made every step painful. But he had a son in elementary school and a daughter in a private middle school. He continued to guide so they could study.

With my composure starting to return, I looked up to the heavens. I'd been on this mountain for six days, and I would not give up. Mount Kilimanjaro stands 19,340 feet above the Tanzania plains, and it proved to be a more formidable challenge than I had expected. My father—my climbing partner on this adventure—appeared to be in a state of exhaustion similar to mine. Our only light to climb by shone from headlamps on this moonless night. The Milky Way seemed to hover inches above our heads in a brilliant, three-dimensional cloud of stars—a sky I'd never seen or imagined. I felt pretty small on this giant mountain under the awesome creation of God.

Three more steps . . . *gasp*. At any moment I expected to break over the crest. The summit continuously eluded us. Three more steps . . . *gasp*. Everything seemed frozen; even time stood still. Six hours deep into what felt like the longest night imaginable, we limped over the steep vertical incline and onto the rim of Kilimanjaro's extinct volcano. In a moment worthy of celebration, we fell to the ground instead. Then all good feelings were quickly extinguished when our guide explained that the real summit—Uhuru Peak—waited "another hour away." Lying in the dirt, I wanted to stop here—this was good enough. But we had come so far that it would be a shame not to finish.

The next two hours were some of the harshest of my life. The air thinned further, and my heart pumped so hard that every step felt like my heart might give out. The sun rose, and the freezing night gave way to searing heat. I looked over the glaciers and way down to our last base camp. Then I looked beyond that to the villages even farther down below. Everything was such a long way away. I felt the farthest from safety I had ever been. There was nothing I could do except keep putting one foot in front of the other.

An hour and a half later, I dropped to my knees in front of a wooden sign that marked our final destination. Pain and exuberance overwhelmed us. We had accomplished the most physically challenging experience either of us had ever set out to do. This was a good feeling—a feeling of intense accomplishment. We had summited into another world—the likes of which only Tolkien or Lewis could dream up. Glaciers rose like ramparts. Pools of water below the glaciers sat so still that I could not tell where the ice began and ended. The crater of the volcano looked like a moonscape, and the clouds surrounding the mountain made us feel as if we were on an island in heaven. We witnessed beauty that few eyes would ever behold.

Seeing What No Human Eye Has Seen

We often condemn adventure as foolhardy, vain, and even purposeless, particularly when we can't account for what we might encounter. We now have "adventure travel" and "adventure racing," as if the idea of adventure is a separate segment of life for wanderers and risk seekers.

Maybe we need more adventure in our lives. As Helen Keller once stated, "Life is either a daring adventure, or nothing."[11] Yet this seeming lack of purpose *is* the purpose—it allows us to open ourselves to the adventure. And adventure is just that—it's exploration and discovery; it's not knowing what's around the next bend, being exposed to the unexpected. Sometimes that is precisely what we need. Adventure often humbles and prepares us for what God wants us to see.

I once took two trips in one summer: on one trip, I knew nothing about my destination. I had flights but had no idea where I would be staying or what I would be doing. On the other, the plans were set in stone to the hour with itineraries, schedules, and photos of accommodations. The first trip changed my life; the second trip left me feeling that there was more I was missing.

It's said that definition is the death of discovery, and the less I know, the more thrilling I find the experience. Though my mind desires to know everything, my soul prefers going to new places, with little information, having read as few maps and guidebooks as possible. The joy of discovery makes me feel as if I am the first person to experience something or someplace.

I've been an avid climber for several years now. In climbing, to have a "first ascent"—to be the first one to climb a mountain—is a notable achievement and an exciting thing. You're privileged to put your name on the route. I don't know whether I've made any true first ascents, but I've climbed routes that few, if any others, have climbed.

To gaze upon what few—or maybe even no other—eyes have seen before is, as director James Cameron puts it, a great fantasy. There's something thrilling about being the first. We want to see for the first time; we want to discover, even if it's only for ourselves. Whether or not we're actually the first, as long as we *might* be the first, there's something special about the experience. I think that's because adventure is wired into us as a major motivator.

To me, adventure is closely linked to art and creativity. I try to dedicate a significant sphere of my life to regular creative activity. For me, that's writing and filmmaking—avenues through which I can tell stories about the world as I experience it. Whenever I start a new blog post, article, or film project, I begin with the tiny seed of an idea. I never know where it will go or into what it will transform. I get more joy out of seeing something take its own shape than I do out of carefully planning a project and trying to meet my own preset expectations.

Can you imagine a greater adventure than Creation? There were no maps, no street signs. God created an entire world from nothing. He brought to life that which had never existed before and allowed it to engage in self-discovery. If we are made in the image of such a great Adventurer, it's no wonder that I'm drawn to places off the map—places where I know no one has visited.

It was adventure and exploration—not knowing what I might find around the next bend—that brought me to new, unexpected places in Thailand and on Kilimanjaro. For me, that place was encountering God. Whether in the faces of the children on Thailand's streets or in the joy of our porters, I found it when I wasn't looking.

An Unexplored Generation

Throughout history, exploration has propelled the human race forward. Yet today I fear that there's little left to explore. There are no more uncharted continents. Nearly the entire globe has been navigated and mapped. There are very few new mountains left to climb. No new oceans left to cross. And, as a result, many of us lose our desire to venture forth.

We now resort to remaking the great expeditions in more and more unusual ways. When early explorers first crossed the Atlantic, it was quite a feat. These days, the vessels are more and more bizarre. The Atlantic has been crossed in a paddleboat; another has crossed in a ship built from junk off the streets of New York City; someone else plans to make the voyage in a one-man, human-powered submarine; and my favorite, still another crossed in a boat made entirely of Popsicle sticks. While I commend these adventurous souls on daring expeditions that I probably will never undertake, they simply don't capture me like the voyages of Leif Eriksson or Christopher Columbus, nor will they live on in the pages of our history books.

On the other hand, anthropologists speculate there are still more than one hundred uncontacted people groups remaining on earth—most are isolated tribes deep in the Amazon or in the jungles of Borneo. The notion that there are still many people in this world living in isolation captures my mind. One such group, the Sentinelese, live on a small remote island in the Indian Ocean. They might be the most isolated group of people in existence, possibly descending directly from the earliest humans and living without contact for thousands of years. They have been observed only from the air, and those who have tried to contact them have never returned.

Exploration, reaching the Sentinelese, often requires delicate anthropological work or expensive technology and, in many cases, considerable debate over ethics: Should we disturb these people? Could we bring them disease? The common response is to let them be.

Overall, we don't see adventure and discovery in our daily news. We don't celebrate exploration as we once did.

Our parents and grandparents had a reason to explore. Many of them watched the first moon landing in 1969. They saw the height of space exploration and this bold new frontier opened up to them. As I was writing this book, NASA retired its space shuttle program, and the United States stepped out of manned space exploration for the foreseeable future. Today's children have no reason to be astronauts anymore—no reason to go to space camp. Unless private companies step in quickly to lift us out of the stratosphere, we will have cut off one of our last outposts in unexplored territory.

There's a strong nexus between faith and exploration. Exploration requires faith. To take the next step, to round the unknown bend, requires a faith that the way forward will sustain you and that you will be able to rise to an unknown challenge. To have faith, you need to explore something unknown and intangible. We don't start our faith with a full understanding of God, we begin with a hint. We ask questions; we wrestle with the answers. To have faith is to look deep into your heart to places where you've never been. You need to explore your soul and what it means to be human.

Faith and exploration bring us back to the labyrinth of life that we all walk. The adventure is what propels us to continue walking even though we don't know where the labyrinth will lead. It sustains us through the wrong turns and forays. It keeps us on watch for those beacons of joy from God.

My first trip to Thailand initially had much more to do with adventure than it did with God's purpose for me. Instead of packing play clothes, I packed climbing shoes. Yet the climbing shoes never left the bag and play clothes were needed at outreach nearly every night. Still, it was the spirit of adventure that had brought me to this new and different life. It's what led me to ask questions and try to find the answers in the slums. That was where my eyes were opened. Exploration took me through turns in the labyrinth I wouldn't normally have made.

It's not surprising to me that some of our greatest explorers were people of deep faith. Marco Polo, David Livingstone, and Ernest Shackleton were compelled to explore, in part, by their faith. I can imagine why. It would have been difficult to be an explorer and not have incredible faith. I can't imagine sailing off in search of new lands while listening to the criticism of others: "There's nothing out there" or "You'll fall off the edge of the world."

So what is left for us? What do we still have to explore? For one thing, we explore cyberspace. The electronic frontier has proved to be new ground for many of us. The age of silicon and semiconductors opened doors to a still-expanding world of seemingly unending opportunities. We can lose ourselves in virtual worlds, alter-ego avatars, and digital stockpiles of information—not always for the better.

We've also turned to exploring one another. Social networks and reality TV allow us to peer into each other's lives as never before. We explore and discover what's on others' minds and in our souls. I remember a few years ago, when Facebook made a controversial change, adding the "News Feed," a real-time listing of the changes people made to their profiles. After the change, when you logged in you saw on one screen all the updates that your friends made. Facebook users were in an uproar. Some expressed concern for privacy reasons, but the most common complaint from those I knew was that they lost the sense of exploration—there was something fun about searching through your friends' profiles to discover what had changed in their lives.

I'm bothered by the feeling that true exploration is largely over. It concerns me that we're left, primarily, to investigate the salacious details of the lives around us. I don't consider that real exploration. Real exploration—true exploration—leads us to believe that the impossible might be true, that there might be inconceivable things out there: wild, untamed places. We are left to imagine what those might be until we can get there. Real exploration gives us a reason to dream.

Now instead of desiring to reach uncharted places, I fear we might be left with desiring what others have. We need to find new places to explore, and we desperately need a new era of exploration.

I wonder if it's in that "vast mutual rescue" that we might find new territory. It's there that we find the places of suffering that are unreached by goodness and God's grace. Maybe this is our new era of exploration.

Bold Dreams

Climbing Kilimanjaro in Africa, I couldn't help but feel a kinship to the early explorers. The trekking teams and porters joined into one long river of people—hundreds of people—making their way through the jungles and up cliffs. The bags on the heads of the porters would bob up and down in a colorful wave like Chinese dragon costumes. I felt as if I were trekking with great explorers such as Dr. David Livingstone. This took little imagination, since trekking through the jungles hasn't changed significantly in the last two centuries. I pictured Livingstone breaking for camp with us every evening. I pictured him sitting in our mess tent sipping tea with us by candlelight.

I didn't know much about Livingstone before our climb began but quickly discovered that our footsteps trailed his long-cast shadow. I often saw landmarks bearing the names of Livingstone and his comrades. Inspired by his mystique, I read books about him and his adventures once I returned home.

This nineteenth-century explorer was part missionary and part adventurer. The two elements seemed to fit together in near-perfect unison as he pursued both simultaneously. And for that, Livingstone was a hero. He was a hero of faith in his homeland of Great Britain, where he had trained as a doctor in Scotland and England and had been sent out by the London Missionary Society. He was also a hero to the scientific elite, receiving significant support from the Royal Geographic Society. The country would wait eagerly for news, which painstakingly made its way from the jungles of Africa via hand-passed letters until finally reaching a telegraph. Once it did, tales of Livingstone's adventures thundered through the streets of London. But he didn't explore for glory, and he didn't explore only for adventure's sake; he explored with a purpose—to build the Kingdom of God.

What I admire the most about Livingstone is that he was bold. His adventures were bold. His convictions were bold. On one of his most daring adventures, he set out to be the first person to walk across Africa. He literally walked, one foot in front of the other, from the Indian Ocean to the Atlantic Ocean. It took him nearly four years.

Livingstone's convictions became bold through what he witnessed. Assembling large caravans to set off into the depths of Africa, he encountered firsthand the vile, growing slave trade. Led by Arab slave traders, caravans even larger than his own frequently passed him, headed in the other direction and leaving the jungle with hundreds of captured Africans chained together. At other times he would stumble upon the corpses of innocent Africans slaughtered in the wake of the slaves. This depraved system incensed Livingstone. He developed an abolitionist's vision to see an end to this immoral trade. It was a bold ambition for his day.

Livingstone's final adventure, and arguably his most courageous, sought to discover the source of the Nile. Finding the fabled source of one of the world's greatest and most important rivers proved to be the ultimate quest for an African explorer. On his quest, Livingstone and his men fought malaria, fever, elephantiasis, mutiny, tribal wars, and even lion attacks. After seventeen years in the jungle, and still yet to achieve this bold dream, he found himself stranded and nearing death in a small tribal village. Seeking the fame attached with finding a now long-missing Livingstone, a swashbuckling Henry Morton Stanley forged his way to the same village. Arriving there, Stanley famously greeted his prize, "Dr. Livingstone, I presume?" Though Stanley would return to Britain and the United States to bring word that Livingstone was alive, Livingstone would never leave the jungle. He died alone in an African village as a hero.

Livingstone's adventures coexisted with a high degree of failure. Yet fear of failure didn't stop him. He sacrificed much for the sake of bold dreams. He lost his wife, Mary, on an expedition to the Zambezi River, where she succumbed to malaria. Even after this, he kept going. He never saw his children again after setting off on his final expedition to Africa. And ultimately, Livingstone never saw his greatest goal achieved: he never discovered the source of the Nile. He passed away from malaria and dysentery not far from the Nile's source. He never saw the abolition of slavery, either.

I wish we had a Livingstone today. He and his compatriots were heroes of faith who embraced bold ideas. He truly embodied the "go and do" spirit. My favorite part of the story is the way his bold vision, though rife with failure, made him come alive. Livingstone was so alive in Africa—alive in his bold vision for a fully explored, Christian Africa—that before ships from the United Kingdom arrived to reclaim Livingstone's body, his African porters removed his heart and buried it in their country.

They buried his heart where they felt it belonged and where he would have wanted it.

Even if I fail, I hope my visions are so bold that my heart will be buried where they have taken me.

Dreaming of a World Restored

Exploring and dreaming share the same spirit. Exploring lets you venture to new places in this world; dreaming lets you venture to new places in your soul. Exploring allows you to see the world as it really is. Dreaming allows you to envision the world as it ought to be—as it's meant to be restored.

When we start to explore, we often uncover a broken world. Like Livingstone, explorers have the opportunity to become restorers. I think God gives us exploration to lead us to restoration. A restored world is the boldest dream we can imagine.

Five hours after our successful climb to the summit of Mount Kilimanjaro, my father and I stumbled back into base camp at fifteen thousand feet. Our team of porters waited there to greet us and celebrate. They had already moved some of our gear down the mountain. The porters amazed us. Getting their job is no easy task. Local Tanzanians wait years for the chance to join a climbing team. If you're lucky enough to become a porter, you work hard to keep your job. Porters carry the gear for their entire team in loads of fifty pounds on their heads—yes, balanced on their heads—then take off, practically sprinting up the mountain in order to set up camp prior to our arrival. Some wear only flip-flops as they climb. They don't get paid well, and it's highly hazardous, with the extreme risk of falling off a cliff because of overexertion. As much as I enjoy climbing mountains, I couldn't make it as a porter, and I doubt I could make it up a mountain without a team of them helping me.

We walked almost the entire way down the mountain, back

into the warm rain forest, for our final night of the expedition. This was an evening to celebrate. Our porters danced and sang for us, overflowing with joy. They sang songs of praise to God in Swahili, and they sang songs of respect for the mountain. The evening was beautiful and energetic.

After the celebration, my father and I sat in the tent discussing how we wanted to say our good-byes to the guides and porters who had served us all week. We knew that the porters made very little money—most of what they survive on is the tips at the end of an expedition. We wanted to tip them well and they deserved it.

The next morning we stepped off Kilimanjaro and drove to the city at the foot of the mountain. Our porters parted from us at the trail end and went home to their families. My father and I went to a hotel, where we left our money in a safe. We asked Godlisten, our guide, if he could round up all the porters so we could say good-bye officially. We drove into town and parked, and Godlisten started making calls on his mobile phone. One by one, each of the porters ambled down the street. They seemed apprehensive, unsure why we would call them back. We thanked them individually for their hard work and gave them their tips. When they saw the amount, they were ecstatic. Word spread to the others, who now came more quickly. Six porters arrived, but one still had not shown up. After another phone call, we learned he was in the shower. As we started getting in the car to leave, he bounded around the corner, hair still wet, running to receive his gift.

Back at the hotel, and to our surprise, Godlisten sat us down and thanked us profusely. With tears in his eyes, he told us that words could hardly describe what we had done for them. We didn't know what we had done, but Godlisten said we were the most meaningful group he had guided. His team knew we actually cared about them—they were not simply porters to us, but had been treated like real people, equal people. It wasn't the tips—though they were icing on the cake—but our being kind and "present" with the team as we all journeyed together.

To this day, when my father and I reflect on our climb to the summit of Mount Kilimanjaro, the physical summit paled in comparison to our real summit. Our favorite story isn't about standing at the top in awe of the wondrous world around us. Our favorite story is about the end, when we thanked our guide and porters. Our reward was the looks on their faces, their surprise when we gave them a personal thank-you and generous tips for their service to us. Memories of the summit have faded, but the image of the porter who ran out of the shower will always stay with us.

A trip that started out all about me and all about adventure—my chance to summit Kilimanjaro—ended up being all about others. We found more joy in touching their lives than in bagging a peak. Building those relationships now feels more heroic than the actual climb. It was an image of a world restored.

Learning to Dream Again

Sometimes I wonder if I'm the only one who still has really outlandish dreams. Not dreams at night—I don't remember most of those—but daydreams. My daydreams are bold. I don't share most of them because I think people would probably say I'm too naive, too idealistic, or at least partially out of my mind.

Though I don't share most of my daydreams, I do share as many ideas as I can—at least the ones that aren't too preposterous. I wish I had the time to put all these ideas into action. I've got pages and pages of them, most of which have never been completed. Yet I think it's a good thing to dream.

Business management expert Gary Hamel, one of the

top business thinkers of our time, created a theory known as "Hamel's Law of Innovation." Based on significant experience and research, Hamel posited, "For every 1,000 ideas, only 100 will have enough commercial promise to merit a small-scale experiment, only ten of those will warrant a substantial financial commitment, and of those, only a couple will turn out to be unqualified successes. It's the inverse log scale behind innovation." In short, Hamel figured that for every thousand ideas, only one actually sticks. Investors, venture capitalists, and inventors follow this general principle. For business strategy, Hamel suggests that "to find one great idea, you must have workers dreaming up thousands."[12]

My family owns a manufacturing firm that conducts considerable amounts of research and development every year. Hamel's law skirts pretty close to the truth. We spend countless hours in the research and development process. Hundreds of product ideas never reach experimentation for proof of concept, much less production. Far fewer products make it to market. Those that find their way into the stream of commerce often fail after a few years. All this is expected. But then, every once in a while, we get a winner, an idea that takes off. Sometimes these one-in-a-thousand products are so successful that they change the course of our business and reshape the market.

Many of us need to learn to dream again. We need to have many, many bold ideas. If we do, every once in a while we'll have dreams that prosper. If we bottle up our dreams or if we keep ourselves from dreaming, then chances are, we will never have even one succeed.

In college I took a required personal-leadership development course. We read books on spiritual development, faith, and, naturally, leadership. One assignment asked us to think about someone from history we admire. We had to write a page or two about the person, then share details about our individual with the class. As the exercise began, everyone had to stand up and tell the class about his or her choice. Most chose respected historical or political figures, humanitarians, or Christian leaders. As each student rose and spoke, the rest of the class nodded in approval and made confirming noises. I started to get a little uneasy—like I had finished the wrong assignment. Finally, the spotlight was on me. I stood up and stated, "I selected Walt Disney." The class erupted in laughter. I explained my choice, sharing how I admired Disney's ability to dream big dreams and be continuously innovative. I'd still make the same choice today.

I once bought an annual pass to Disneyland. When I purchased the pass, I didn't have anyone in particular to go with me. But I figured that if I had it, I might take guests.

Standing in line at the ticket booth, I started to feel self-conscious. I wasn't sure if, at my age, I should be buying an annual pass to Disneyland. Then I entered the park and remembered how much I loved its wonderment and magic. Other than places like this, there's not much room for dreams anymore.

We all need a place like Disneyland, a place where anything is possible and whatever we can dream up just might happen. We need room to explore ourselves and share our 999 lousy ideas without fear of rejection or failure. These are the places where bold ideas take shape, where we begin to come alive, where our personal revolution ignites, and where world-changing stories start to unfold.

CHAPTER 8

The Great Tension

WE EACH BECOME A COLLECTION of other people's desires for our lives. In my life, I've coined a phrase to describe the tug I often feel between who I want to be and who I'm expected to be. I call this the "Great Tension." It's the tension between this collection of other people's desires for my life and God's desire for my life. It's a tension between what I'm supposed to do and what I dream of doing.

Take a minute right now to think about the collection of other people's desires that you have become. Or think about the collection of people's desires that you *could* have become had others been able to control your life. It can be overwhelming. Friends, family, professors, employers, loan officers, landlords, mobile phone companies, etc. They all desire something from your life. Some have only the best of intentions, while others want to use you as a tool for their desires.

I have had many students come to my office excited to "go and do" one day, then reluctant the next. Why? "My parents are nervous," one student explains. "I was told this won't help me get a job," says another, or "I should stay here and earn money." Those who decline the opportunity to "go" rarely do so of their own volition. Rather, it's because of other people's expectations of their lives. They haven't found something that would make them happier, but someone wasn't happy with their choices.

The Great Tension, this collection of other people's desires for our lives versus what we want, can be a powerful force. If we're not careful, it can control us, halt us in our tracks, and pull us away from God's direction for our lives.

Jesus' Journey through the Desert

The desert that I wandered through was a sort of tension with temptations and the pressures of other people's desires. The expectations of my chosen education were that I should spend my summers working in a law firm. People close to me questioned whether I was making the right decision to go to Thailand and suggested that a more traditional approach might be more practical. Then there was my vision of the heroic, my desire for an adventure to "go and do." These expectations were pitted against following God's beacon. I found myself halted on my labyrinth—in a very dry place.

Thankfully, in deserts we are not alone. Jesus wandered through the desert too. He wandered through a real desert for forty days and forty nights. It's a story known as the "Temptation of Jesus," and it's shared in the gospels of Matthew, Mark, and Luke. Despite the name given to the story, the "temptation" of Jesus might be a bit of a misnomer. "Temptation" might be more properly interpreted as "testing"; the context of the story supports that understanding.

Jesus was led into the desert by the Holy Spirit for his test—not by the devil, not by a trick, but purposely by God. Matthew presents the scenes that unfold as three prearranged tests for Jesus. Overall, the tests described in the fourth chapter of Matthew are set up as a journey Jesus had to take in order to solidify his role as the Son of God and demonstrate his humanity.

The first test that Jesus faced presented the opportunity to fulfill his needs on his own. After wandering the desert for forty days and forty nights, he was hungry. The devil told him, "If you are the Son of God, tell these stones to become loaves of bread." Despite the offer, Jesus refused to turn the stones into bread.

For his second test, the tables were turned and Jesus received the opportunity to test God. The devil took Jesus to the pinnacle of the Temple in the Holy City and told him to throw himself off. "If you are the Son of God, jump off! For the Scriptures say, 'He will order his angels to protect you. And they will hold you up with their hands so you won't even hurt your foot on a stone.'" Jesus again refused, responding, "The Scriptures also say, 'You must not test the LORD your God.'"

Finally, the devil tested Jesus with power and riches. He took Jesus to a high mountain where they could see all the kingdoms of the world and all their glory. If Jesus would bow down and worship the devil, these things would all be his. "I will give it all to you," the devil offered, "if you will kneel down and worship me." Jesus again refused. "'Get out of here, Satan,' Jesus told him. 'For the Scriptures say, "You must worship the LORD your God and serve only him."'" The devil went away, and the angels returned for Jesus. He had "passed" his final exam.

I imagine this was a wild journey for Jesus as the devil accompanied him through these three tests. They walked out of the wilderness, ascended to the highest point of the Temple in the Holy City, then climbed to the top of a mountain. These tests were each a journey in themselves—the culmination of a larger forty-day journey through the desert.

Pushing Onward

Understanding how Jesus was tested in the desert gives us perspective. Knowing that throughout life we go in and out of deserts helps us to anticipate these deserts and prepares us to deal with them. This understanding reminds us that the wilderness will not last; we just need to push through. We know there's something better on the other end.

I find it interesting that God tested Jesus in the first place. When Jesus entered the desert, he was already the chosen one. There was no competition. The Holy Spirit descended on Jesus at his baptism and immediately led him into the desert. There was a commitment. God could not have feared that Jesus would fail the tests. It asks the question, why test Jesus at all? I can only conclude that this had to, unequivocally, be part of the journey. Before Jesus could get to the "go" part or the "do" part of his work on earth, he had to be tested. And so it is with us.

These deserts strike me, then, as "rites of passage."

A few years after my initial desert wandering, I found myself again in a shorter, but similar, desert when I studied for the bar exam. Preparing for this one exam involved two months of all-day summer prep courses, then studying all evening. It was exhausting and, as if life was repeating itself, discouraging. Practice exams were a struggle, and the expectations of everyone and all the money I'd spent on my education hung in the balance. And, this time, it all hung on one giant two-day exam.

Not everyone who goes to law school has to take the bar exam. You can finish with your Juris Doctor degree and call it a day. But you can't practice law unless you finish the journey. The bar exam is part of that journey. And for the most part, everyone who goes to an accredited law school should be able to pass the exam. What it comes down to is that the bar exam is simply a rite of passage—you have to make sacrifices, work hard, and pass the exam. It doesn't even matter how well you score; you only have to pass. As I was going through the desert of studying for the bar exam, I thought a lot about Jesus going through his desert. I didn't want to be in the desert; I wanted to turn stones into bread. But I knew it would be over soon enough, and I could continue the journey. I could finally get to the "do" part.

While I don't like deserts in life, I now have an appreciation for them. I see them as guideposts—if we're in a desert, it might mean we are being prepared for something better.

Deserts come in many forms: failed goals, loneliness, sickness, to name a few. My wife, Lisa, went through a desert of her own a few years before we were married. She had trained for years for the Olympic windsurfing team and had tried out for the sole woman's spot on the American team. In the midst of all this, she was diagnosed with—and beat—thyroid cancer. When she didn't clinch the sole spot, she had to decide whether to spend another four years chasing the dream or to finish nursing school. She wandered in a desert for a while before determining that serving others as a nurse brought her true and sustained joy.

I might even go so far as to say that a desert can be a gift. But we often realize this only in hindsight. If I hadn't failed those exams early in law school, I wouldn't have wandered into the first desert. I wouldn't have asked myself, *What am I doing here?* I wouldn't have challenged conventional wisdom, and I likely would have followed tempting offers that came my way.

I know I'm on the right path if I'm sensing internal tension. If you're following God's beacon and you're being prepared for something larger, you will feel resistance. Deserts are opportunities to give pause and realize we must change how we handle our own great tension.

Balancing Tension

The key is not in eliminating tension, but in how we manage it. Is tension necessarily a bad thing? In a system of desires that pull our lives in opposite directions, a little tension holds our lives together. It's all about how you load and balance the system.

I've learned a lot about life from rock climbing. In the sport of climbing, the foundational principles involve building rope and anchor systems. The most important element in those systems is tension. Before you literally hang your life on the line, you need to create some anchor points.

The first step involves setting your anchors—usually three or more. You want to build your anchor on solid rock—something that's not going to give way. Once you have hitched yourself steadfast, you tie one connecting rope to all three. This rope is your lifeline—you're hanging off the end.

The three anchors want to pull your system in different directions. If you tie to only one anchor, you're at high risk of an accident—the entire load is placed on one anchor, and if it blows, you have no second chance. Instead, you want to load all three anchors so that they spread the weight evenly among each one, effectively providing backup for each other. The key to this system is tension. The rope binding all the anchors needs to have adequate tension to keep the system together. If you build the system properly, you have equal tension among all anchors and also a minimal amount of tension on any one anchor. While you're climbing, a properly tensioned system is the most secure system.

In life as in climbing, it's easy to go to the extreme and completely give in to one desire—one anchor. For instance, some people give up family, friends, and other responsibilities to "go and do." It's an admirable commitment and an effective method for managing desires—essentially eliminating them—but it's poorly tensioned. In such a system, completely giving in to one desire leaves you hanging from only one anchor. It's a dangerous system, subject to collapse.

For me, the climb is an ascent toward God and getting to his desires for my life. My anchors include family, friends, my work with the Global Justice Program, and my personal go and do projects. When I was in the desert, I was hanging nearly everything on my then anchor of school, and the tension was killing me. I had lost touch with friends and I was frustrated. Now I feel more properly balanced. Still, it would be easy to hang everything from one anchor again. At times, I've felt like work was overwhelming the balance. Visualizing my life as a tensioned system has helped me find the right balance.

So while tension can be seen as negative, it can actually be a good thing. Tension holds the system together; it holds our lives in balance. We need to find anchors formed into solid rock—just as the wise man built his house upon rock. Anchors consist of our responsibilities—careers, families, education—and our opportunities to "go and do." I believe our job is to build a properly tensioned system that can hold our responsibilities in balance with opportunities to "go and do."

"Go and do" is not a zero-sum game. We don't have to hang our lives on one anchor in order to go and do. We certainly need individuals who are willing to make huge sacrifices to serve. I, however, don't find it realistic for the majority of us. It's more realistic to envision a properly tensioned life system.

In fact, those who put everything on a go and do anchor can be misled. Students frequently visit my office with an interest in serving the "least of these" around the world, but they worry it means they must commit to a career in global jus-tice—what they see as a one-anchor life. They've watched the celebrations and fanfare surrounding their peers who put it all on one anchor, and they start to believe that's the only way. This is misguided.

Some people do have the privilege of spending an entire lifetime going and doing in one particular place, whether that's in full-time mission work or full-time devotion to a particular "mission" at work or at home. But for the rest of us, "go and do" should be a part of our lifestyle, part of a commitment balanced in tension with other significant commitments. I would like to see everyone develop a passionate perseverance to serve a hurt-ing world, go and do as soon as possible, and then return home to make it part of a long-term personal vision.

From my post at a university, I believe that focusing on a mass of graduates with "go and do" lifestyles will pay greater dividends than focusing solely on the small handful of gradu-ates who will make it their careers.

Parallel Careers

So how exactly do we balance all of this? We need to find "par-allel careers." Management guru Peter Drucker observed cor-porate executives burning out around age forty from boredom. Finding this age to be the tipping point, Drucker divided our lives into two distinct halves: what we do until forty and what we do after forty.

To avoid burnout, Drucker suggested preparing for the "second half" of life—what we will do after forty—well before we get there. Drucker proposed creating a "parallel career" for the second half, such as working for a nonprofit, starting a foundation, or finding a meaningful side project.

I agree with Drucker that we should have a parallel career.

But I wonder why we must wait for the second half of life. Why not create a meaningful parallel career as soon as possible?

Drucker made an important finding: when people do not start volunteering early in their lives, they never do. As he puts it, "If one does not begin to volunteer before one is forty or so, one will not volunteer past sixty."[13] Clearly, the first half of your life is critical.

Congresswoman Shirley Chisholm once said, "Service to others is the rent you pay for your room here on earth."[14] We're like that older brother still crashing on his parents' couch in his forties—if we don't start paying rent now, we likely never will.

I'm always inspired and encouraged when students come to my office ready to begin something. Even if their ideas are unsuccessful, I know that because the students were ready to start once, they will most likely try again. Just recently, I was visited by two young ladies who wanted to combine their passion for fashion with their inspiration from microfinance. Whether it works or doesn't is less important than trying. With working-life expectancies on the rise and delays in retirement, "later" is becoming less of an option.

Thankfully, great role models exist who inspire us to find the balance to "go and do." The people who inspire me the most are not people like Gandhi and Mother Teresa. I admire them, but to tell the truth, they don't inspire me.

Admiration and inspiration are different concepts. To admire, dictionary defined, is to regard with wonder. To inspire is to be filled with an animating, exalting influence. These heroes of humanitarianism fill me with wonder, but it's harder for me to be filled with animating influence by them. The reason there aren't more of them is that few people can do what they do—they are outliers. Their rarity is what makes them so special. Their sacrifices and efforts are extraordinary, and we have much to learn from them. However, for the majority of us, it's an unrealistic model. I'll never be a Gandhi or a Mother Teresa.

I'm more encouraged by those at the median than by the fringe. People who have successfully found balance are an animating, exalting influence on me. They inspire me because they live the kinds of lives that I can emulate. I can be like them. They demonstrate that the go and do lifestyle can be lived by every man or woman.

I think about some of the people who most inspire me. Many found parallel careers in the first part of their lives. Some have started nonprofit companies to pursue their passions. As soon as their day jobs are over, they rush home to work on their passions, or they work on them from ten to midnight after they put their kids to bed. One friend is dedicated to feeding and serving the homeless in Malibu. He spends his weekends making sandwiches and fellowshipping with them. Another friend realized that nearly all organizations fighting human trafficking focused on women, yet there were many boys also abused. She started a shelter and rehabilitation program. Another set of friends decided to support and expand a home for orphaned boys in Africa. All of these individuals come alive in their parallel careers.

So how do we get to a place where we can go and do? We must identify and handle the great tensions in our lives. We must manage the expectations of others, not so that they control us, but so that we find balance. Once we do this, we've found the key to unlocking the go and do lifestyle.

CHAPTER 9

The Power of Presence

"HI, JAY. Can I ask you a question about the trip?" Jennifer's head poked around the corner of my office door.

Jennifer was signed up to join a spring break trip that I was leading to refugee camps along the Burmese border. She was one of the students I was most looking forward to taking because this trip fell so far outside her comfort zone. Whenever I saw Jennifer, she was always dressed to the max: high heels, designer dresses, and perfect hair. Her only foray out of the United States had been a trip to Paris staying in five-star hotels with her parents. Fighting for human rights in developing countries might be quite possibly the furthest thing from what she wanted to do with her life. Jennifer would be graduating in a few months and planned to be an intellectual property lawyer, so she would be sitting in tall office buildings advising high-profile clients on patents and trademarks. Yet something had inclined her heart to go on this trip while she had the chance.

I already knew what she would ask me. I could see it coming, because I get this all the time. A grin always breaks across my face when I hear this question from a student—or anyone, really. My answer was ready before she even asked.

"What are we going to do there?" Jennifer timidly asked. Apparently the fact that we would board a plane in a month caught up with the thrill of committing to "go." She suddenly realized she didn't have a clear picture of what we would accomplish with our time. Little did she know that neither did I.

"It doesn't matter!" I replied. I threw my hands up in the air to add a little emphasis.

Jennifer looked stunned. She didn't know what to say. My answer was not what she expected to hear; it's not what anyone expects to hear, for that matter. Jennifer, like most people who ask this question, wanted an itinerary, an agenda, and a goal. Jennifer wanted action. As a society we've become accustomed to always doing something, but we've burdened the meaning of "something." We've been led to believe that "something" requires action, that there must be a concrete goal and metrics by which to measure its success. We set expectations. We believe we must return with drastically different before and after photos in order to make our time legitimate.

Somehow we've created a distinction between "doing" and "being." That distinction is wrong, very wrong. We need to reevaluate what it means to "do" and realize that simply being present is as significant as any grand project—possibly even more so.

The concept of being present is nothing new. One prophetic voice for presence was renowned priest and author

Henri J. Nouwen, who wrote profusely on spirituality. One of his topics referred to "the ministry of presence":

> More and more, the desire grows in me simply to walk around, greet people, enter their homes, sit on their doorsteps, play ball, throw water, and be known as someone who wants to live with them. It is a privilege to have the time to practice this simple ministry of presence. Still, it is not as simple as it seems. My own desire to be useful, to do something significant, or to be part of some impressive project is so strong that soon my time is taken up by meetings, conferences, study groups, and workshops that prevent me from walking the streets. It is difficult not to have plans, not to organize people around an urgent cause, and not to feel that you are working directly for social progress. But I wonder more and more if the first thing shouldn't be to know people by name, to eat and drink with them, to listen to their stories and tell your own, and to let them know with words, handshakes, and hugs that you do not simply like them, but truly love them.[15]

Nouwen's words tug at my deepest desires. We all have the intense desire to do something significant or be a part of an impressive project. We want to accomplish grand things that we can write about in our memoirs. Yet I'm not sure we're necessarily supposed to do grand or significant things. I think we make the world a better place just by being present.

A month after my meeting with Jennifer, we joined a small team of law students for a couple of days in a Burmese refugee camp. We didn't change the life of a single refugee. We didn't improve anything at the camp. If I showed you before and after photos, you would see no difference. But we were present. We went to church in the camp—and we each shared with the congregation about our lives. We broke bread with the people living there. Then we sat for hours in a bamboo hut that served as a dormitory for orphaned teenagers. These teenagers, all refugees, told us their stories. Most had not seen their parents for years, in many cases since the night a battalion of the Burma Army attacked their village. Everyone ran into the jungles, and families separated amid the turmoil. The teens sang us songs—songs of hope and despair. We even sang a song for them. When it was time to go, a group of teenagers followed us all the way to the entrance of the camp to wave good-bye.

Our team of law students piled into the van, and as soon as the door slammed shut, Jennifer spun around with a look of pure joy on her face. "Wow! That was more than I ever imagined it could be!" She had seen the beauty of presence.

What's Right in Front of You

A few years later, I met an international volunteer who had spent a small amount of time with Mother Teresa. He told her that he felt overwhelmed with all the needs in the world and sought her counsel. "How do you decide what to do?" he asked.

Mother Teresa replied, "You just do what's in front of you."

We always want to know what to do. We need agendas, plans, and goals. Not having the security of a schedule or goal is one of the biggest roadblocks preventing people from going. Yet some of the most effective accomplishments we can make are the ones we can't anticipate—it's what we find right in front of us. We need to worry less about what we are going to do and more about our willingness to start showing up. When we're satisfied that we are being present, we most often discover what we're really meant to do.

When I think about presence, I think about outreach in Thailand. Outreach was about showing up on the street to just play with kids or talk to mothers. It was about walking around, sitting on steps, playing ball—there were no grand schemes of significance. We did whatever was right in front of us.

Presence starts with simply showing up. If I could make one recommendation to anyone thinking about going, it would be this: don't overthink it; just show up. Once you're there—once you're present—the pieces fall into place.

Sometimes, it's all about showing up—especially when no one else will. I once led a team to Uganda with the purpose of building legal cases for children detained in one of the country's prisons. Accused of a crime, these kids had not yet received their day in court. Many of them were innocent, and the evidence to convict them did not exist. In other cases, though the children had committed petty crimes, they were still sitting in jail. They had slipped through the cracks.

When we finished our few days of building their cases and prepared to depart, one of the children approached us. He said, "Thank you for what you're doing for us, but even if you can't help us, thank you for showing up." No one else had showed up.

Speaking as a lawyer from a Western, developed nation, I should be able to solve almost every problem I encounter, according to my instincts, anyway. That, however, is not always the case—sometimes legal systems fail to function properly and a problem can't be easily resolved. In these instances, simply being present can be the only thing we can do—and the most meaningful.

Not only should we show up but we must also continue to show up again and again. I regularly return to Thailand and Uganda for the purpose of being present. I don't necessarily have a purpose beyond that, nor do I even know what I'll do once I'm there. I try to return regularly to let people know that we're still with them, that we haven't forgotten them. When I depart, those I say good-bye to can count on the fact that I will be coming back to see them.

I'm continually challenged to balance the desire to go everywhere with my commitment to consistently return to some of the same places in order to be present. Every time I travel to Thailand or Uganda, I know I could be checking many other countries off my list of "Countries I Visited and Helped." Nevertheless, I fell in love with the people in Thailand and Uganda, and I have no choice but to return regularly.

One King James Version of the Bible

It took me awhile to embrace the idea of presence. I used to need agendas, plans, and schedules too. I've come a long way, but I know I will always be a student of presence.

On a trip into Burma, I spent a morning at a tiny orphanage up in the hills. Pastor James and his wife ran the orphanage as well as a church in the nearby village. Another man arrived that morning—Pastor Thomas, a Burmese gentleman who appeared to be Pastor James's superior. Pastor Thomas described himself as a regional pastor who oversaw many Christian churches in this part of Burma.

Over the course of the morning, I started asking Pastor James some questions, speaking with him alone while Pastor Thomas was engaged in another conversation on the other side of the room. I explained that I had traveled from the United States, where I was a lawyer, and worked for a law school in the States. I shared that my areas of work included international human rights. He understood.

"Then you know about the government in Burma?" Pastor

James asked in a hushed voice, his eyes darting around the room as though someone might be listening to us.

"Yes," I confirmed, knowing he couldn't say too much out loud. Burma reminded me of Narnia under the control of the evil White Witch, where even the trees are spies. "I know a lot about the government."

Pastor James nodded approvingly.

I asked if there was anything I could do to help him or help the situation in Burma. Pastor James called to Pastor Thomas, pulling him from his separate conversation. The two men stood in the middle of the room, speaking to each other in Burmese. They soon turned back to me.

Pastor James turned to me. "Can you get us one English version of the King James Bible?"

I stood in disbelief.

This orphanage had no supporters and no donors. Pastor James and his wife lived in constant fear that the government might shut them down because they were affiliated with the Christian church. Support money for the orphanage could have gone a long way, but here he was asking me for one Bible.

When my shock subsided, I told the men that I actually had an English copy of the New International Version with me. It might not be the version they wanted, but I would be happy to leave it with them. They were thrilled.

My small gesture held greater significance than I could understand at the moment. In Burma, religious freedom exists in the constitution, but fails to exist in practice. The military junta controls everything tightly. The "Burmese Way of Socialism" adopted in the 1990s set out a campaign encouraging, essentially requiring, Buddhism. The nation, run at the behest of fortune-tellers and astrologers who advise its dictators, heavily restricts religious materials, especially Christian resources. Only one state-approved version of the Bible is available, and even that has a list of censored words removed. I was told it was illegal to even possess a Bible printed outside of Burma.

When I pulled out my NIV, the pastors performed a small ceremony, complete with photos and signatures, where I handed the Bible over to the regional pastor in a formal manner. They grinned from ear to ear and lavished me with thank-yous.

I had visited the orphanage simply to be present with the kids for a few hours. I didn't know I would talk to anyone about the Burma situation. I didn't come with an agenda. I spent time with Pastor James and his family for a few hours—I ate with them, and I built their trust. Had I not been present that afternoon, I would have missed their immediate need. In this instance, the need didn't involve overthrowing the government or funding an orphanage; it was merely sharing a Bible they could not otherwise obtain. Presence won the day.

An Appeal for Presence

On a cool spring night in Lima, Peru, I crossed a busy street with a team of law students in tow. We stood on the sidewalk outside what appeared to be an abandoned warehouse in San Juan de Lurigancho, Lima's poorest and roughest neighborhood. The warehouse front boasted a large metal garage door. We wondered whether this was the right destination. Suddenly, a small hinged door swung open from the middle of the garage as if we had stumbled upon a secret entrance. Ducking as we stepped through the door, we stood in what appeared to be an abandoned warehouse. Walls were unfinished and metal girders lay on the floor. A few construction workers looked away from their projects for a moment, but then turned right back to their welding and pounding.

We were supposed to meet with high school and college

students at a church. This was no church, and not a student was in sight. A middle-aged Peruvian man with a mullet appeared, acting like he was expecting us and motioning for us to follow him. We stepped across some corrugated metal, around a ladder, and then up three flights of stairs. The stairs spilled into a large, open, carpeted room with folding chairs and dozens of young people in their late teens and early twenties. On this floor it was, indeed, a church.

The man with the mullet explained that the students met here regularly of their own volition. For the last few months, they had met weekly to study an educational module on justice. A justice-focused group called Paz y Esperanza organized the module. The takeaway from the program: students must create an action plan for justice and then go into their communities and act on those plans. That night was the final group meeting.

Many of the students came from the hills surrounding Lima. They lived in Lima's sprawling "human settlements," hillsides dotted with colorful shanty homes. Decades ago, thousands of Peru's indigenous people were displaced in a civil war against a terrorist group called the Shining Path. Many of the indigenous people were accused of associating with the terrorist group. Some were imprisoned, some lost their land, and some were murdered. After a couple decades, many of Peru's youth were without homes, practically refugees in their own country.

In these human settlements narrow, dusty footpaths wind up steep hills. One wrong step might send you tumbling down a steep mountainside. Houses are built with scavenged timber, corrugated cardboard for the sidewalls, and black garbage bags that attempt to keep out the rain. The dire conditions are disheartening.

That night, the students sat in small groups as they prepared to summarize what they'd learned through the justice module.

The final activity required each group to define "justice" as they understood it, representing the word *justice* on a hand-drawn poster.

The first group of students rose and unfurled their poster. A large globe occupied the center of the paper, flanked on each side by a person. These figures stood tall, shaking hands above the globe. The students pointed to one of the hand-drawn people and said that this represented us—our group of American law students. Then they pointed to the other person and said that this person represented the South American teens. They told us that justice was all of us meeting together. Though we came from wealth and they came from poverty, justice was all of us being together and getting along. Our presence that night embodied their vision of justice. It meant something to them that we were there.

From the Bible that I gave the Burmese pastors to the Peruvian students studying biblical justice, I started to think more about presence. I thought about how frequently we overlook it. Presence is an important yet underappreciated concept in the Bible. Some of God's most powerful attributes are expressed through his presence. We find joy in his presence (see Psalm 16:11; Acts 2:28). The earth trembles at his presence (Nahum 1:5). God often chooses presence to accomplish his goals.

Then I thought about the many prayers in church or small groups where we invoke God's presence ("Lord, we know you are present with us"). We find comfort in presence.

There's something powerful about being present. Through presence, we are able to encounter the true and living God. Today, we comprehend the power of the crowd more than at any time before. We live in an era where fortunes are built on the number of hits a website might receive. Homegrown heroes are made by how many views they get on YouTube. Nobodies become celebrities. The power of the crowd teaches us that together we are stronger than when we are individuals. And with today's current technology, it's easier than ever to find an outlet for your message. If the collective crowd can adopt something—any cause, any idea, any lifestyle—it becomes a force to be reckoned with.

A crowd can show us another important thing: we are all very small. When you're part of the crowd and you look around, it can be hard to feel significant. We all want to feel significant, but when we're overwhelmed by the odds, we often find ourselves with a difficult choice: we can give up and fade into the ether of life, or we can try to chase something more.

Rather than chase significance, most of us chase participation. We aren't seeking fame or Nobel Peace Prizes. I didn't go across the world with the goal of *solving* human trafficking. I just wanted to know I had done something about it. If someone asks me today about modern-day slavery, I can reply, "Yes, I know. I was there, and I did what I could to help."

I think that we all simply want to know that we were present and that we participated in life. From my own experience, if I could make life better for just one person, I find that to be significant. I think I've been significant to Song and Faifah, and that's been a joy to me. Numbers don't matter; it's about individuals. I'm an individual, so I identify with individuals. I can imagine their suffering and picture how significant it would be to me if someone rescued me.

Although we might not set out to change the world, the reality is that people *do* change the world.

People are the only ones who *can* change the world.

Change is a great thing, but as we've already seen, it can't be our driving force. We have to be motivated by something bigger than our own achievements. We must be willing to accept that though our contributions may be small, they are nonetheless significant to someone. We must be content with fractions and moments.

Getting Caught in the Moment

I'm exhausted tonight. My last two days have been nonstop for twelve to fifteen hours. I've been hosting a delegation of African judges at Pepperdine. We make sure that every detail of their day is planned from breakfast until they return to their hotels after dinner. Although I'm tired—and the fatigued part of me wishes I had never extended the invitation in the first place—I speculate that I will one day look back on these visits and conversations with awe and wonder. Sometimes (especially when things are exhausting) it's hard for us to see things clearly in the moment.

Among the visitors I've hosted, some have included the Chief Justice—the father of Uganda's constitution; the deputy chief justice—one of the first women lawyers in Uganda and a true pioneer in the legal profession; and the minister of justice from Rwanda—who directly advises the president.

Over lunch today, we held conversations in our law school conference room about enhancing African legal systems. The greatest challenge in Africa is a lack of resources—both financial and human. As a result, these rather young judicial systems must be quick; open minded; and, most of all, innovative.

At our table, the Ugandan justices were considering decisions that would dramatically change how the justice system is made available to 40 million people. These were the top in command of the judicial branch that held the power to remold a nation. It was as if we were sitting down with America's founding fathers to talk about how America's system of government might be designed.

It hit me later how important these conversations could be. There's a caution about getting caught up in the moment and losing sight of the bigger picture. Other times, we have the opposite problem. We get so overwhelmed by the big picture that we lose the moment. We miss how incredible small meetings or details can be.

When the chief justice of Uganda visited, I spent a week driving him around the Los Angeles area—including a visit to Disneyland. As the father of Uganda's constitution (he penned it himself), he looms large as an international legal giant. This delegation reminded me how unique that moment was. One of the judges told me how few Ugandans can say they had the privilege of driving the chief justice. *Wow,* I thought for a moment, *I did drive the chief justice.* And I didn't just drive him around—we rode roller coasters together!

These are moments I want to remember: when I was a fly on the wall for a world-shaping conversation or I was privileged to drive the leader of a nation. While nation-shaping moments don't happen every day, other spectacular moments do. My wife, Lisa, had to point out the brilliant pink-flowering tree that I ducked under every day coming into our apartment. It's marvelous, but I had missed it for the bigger picture.

I need to get caught up in the moment more often because, ultimately, being present is about being in the moment.

CHAPTER 10

Use Words If Necessary

"I NEED TO TALK TO YOU," said Michelle as she confronted me in the hallway one afternoon. I could tell by her tone and the scowl on her face that she was upset.

We had finished a presentation in which our law students shared recent "go and do" experiences. Michelle had committed to go to an Asian country over the summer to work directly with victims of human trafficking. Another student, Terri, did similar work in Africa and Asia with trafficking victims the previous two summers. Terri spent significant amounts of time volunteering abroad and domestically. She traveled the world working for orphanages and human rights organizations. I wanted Michelle and Terri to meet—and they did that day—but apparently the introduction had not gone smoothly.

"So, what's wrong?" I asked. "Didn't you get to talk to Terri for a few minutes?"

"Yes," Michelle responded. "I asked her what you say to a victim of human trafficking. All she said was, 'You just give her a hug.' What kind of answer is that?!"

"Maybe she's right," I replied.

Michelle turned her head and stormed off. She wanted words to say—a script of advice and spiritual counsel to give. She wanted a message she could prepare to share with a victim. Even with all her experience, Terri didn't have any of those things to offer.

That summer came and went. Three months after the sensitive interaction between Michelle and Terri, Michelle stopped by my office to tell me about her "go and do" summer. She had been in Asia, interning with an organization that assists victims of human trafficking through housing, aftercare, training, and rehabilitation. She lived with twenty-five women recovering from trafficking.

"Remember that conversation we had in the hallway after you met Terri last spring?" I asked Michelle. "Terri told you that sometimes all you can do for victims of trafficking is give them a hug. What do you think about that now?"

Michelle smiled sheepishly and chuckled. "She was absolutely right."

Preaching the Gospel

A friend of mine works for Opportunity International, a successful and respected microfinance organization modeled after Jesus' call to love and serve the poor. Opportunity International gives microloans to entrepreneurs in developing countries to help them start businesses. Opportunity does not evangelize in the traditional sense—it doesn't preach the gospel at its meetings or require borrowers to learn about Jesus before getting a loan. As my friend told me, "Through Opportunity's process of giving loans, it's the first time many of our clients see God's love for them." Opportunity evangelizes through its actions, and it reaches huge numbers of people who see the love of God for the first time—people unaccustomed to having authentic acts done for them.

I love the quote commonly attributed to St. Francis of Assisi: "Preach the Gospel at all times and when necessary use words." As I learned, "go and do" is not something from which you can easily walk away. Once I went, I couldn't turn off that part of me. It became not an event or a trip, but a lifestyle. It started to alter the way I lived and the way I looked at the world. If one motto describes the "go and do" lifestyle, this phrase associated with Assisi might be it. We preach the gospel, even shout the gospel, but if you're not watching, you might not catch it.

The issues that capture our hearts and minds frequently encompass the most tragic events in this world: intense poverty, genocide, slavery—you name it. Despite the intensity of these matters, I find that to "do" effectively, I must use words infrequently. Instead of speaking, I hug. I play with kids. I show up. I'm present. As the old adage goes, "Actions speak louder than words." Often our actions represent the first time others will see God's love for them, and through these actions, the Word of God may be spoken loudly.

Being Served as Service

As I mentioned earlier, the idea of "doing" often connotes action and movement—if we're not acting, we think we're not accomplishing.

This culture predisposes us to seeing service as action— "acts" of service. We want to parachute in and help take care of things for others. But God's reverse economy doesn't always work this way. Maybe we need to allow people to serve us more often. I know, it sounds strange and counterintuitive, but consider the story of the sinful woman who anointed Jesus:

One of the Pharisees asked Jesus to have dinner with him, so Jesus went to his home and sat down to eat. When a certain immoral woman from that city heard he was eating there, she brought a beautiful alabaster jar filled with expensive perfume. Then she knelt behind him at his feet, weeping. Her tears fell on his feet, and she wiped them off with her hair. She kept kissing his feet and putting perfume on them.

When the Pharisee who had invited him saw this, he said to himself, "If this man were a prophet, he would know what kind of woman is touching him. She's a sinner!"

Then Jesus answered his thoughts. "Simon," he said to the Pharisee, "I have something to say to you."

"Go ahead, Teacher," Simon replied.

Then Jesus told him this story: "A man loaned money to two people—500 pieces of silver to one and 50 pieces to the other. But neither of them could repay him, so he kindly forgave them both, canceling their debts. Who do you suppose loved him more after that?"

Simon answered, "I suppose the one for whom he canceled the larger debt."

"That's right," Jesus said. Then he turned to the woman and said to Simon, "Look at this woman kneeling here. When I entered your home, you didn't offer me water to wash the dust from my feet, but she has washed them with her tears and wiped them with her hair. You didn't greet me with a kiss, but from the time I first came in, she has not stopped kissing my feet. You neglected the courtesy of olive oil to anoint my head, but she has anointed my feet with rare perfume. I tell you, her sins—and they are many—have been forgiven, so she has shown me much love. But a person who is forgiven little shows only little love."

Then Jesus said to the woman, "Your sins are forgiven."

The men at the table said among themselves, "Who is this man, that he goes around forgiving sins?"

And Jesus said to the woman, "Your faith has saved you; go in peace."

LUKE 7:36-50

The story of Jesus and the sinful woman presents a profound example of grace and forgiveness. The story gives many people the courage to enter difficult situations and be with those who have large debts to cancel. Jesus overcame external conflict by breaking with deep-rooted traditions in allowing a prostitute to kiss his feet, wash them with her tears and hair, and pour perfume on them. Then, Jesus offered the woman forgiveness. It's a bold scene.

I find two things interesting about this story. First, Jesus was relaxing—he reclined at the table. He was not teaching, healing, turning water into wine, or driving out demons (any of which could have been useful in this setting). Rather, he was simply being present with a Pharisee by having dinner in his home. We frequently focus on Jesus' actions in the Gospels. We cite fewer examples of Jesus simply hanging out and ministering through presence.

Second, I find it intriguing to consider what Jesus could have done. In law there's a theory called "acts of omission." Acts of omission—things people do not do—are sometimes as relevant as what they do. I'd apply the same principle here when considering Jesus' acts. What didn't he do?

If I had been Luke, the doctor who assembled this Gospel through years of research, I might have wanted to write the story much differently. I might have wished that Jesus had stopped the woman as soon as her tears touched his feet. Then, I'd create a scene similar to the one where the woman who bled for years touched Jesus' cloak and Jesus stopped everything to turn around and acknowledge her for her faith. I'd use that same powerful action. Now the plot would thicken—Jesus would take the perfume and pour it on the sinful woman's feet in an act of respect. I imagine a scene similar to Jesus washing his disciples' feet at the Last Supper. My version would turn the tables, and the literary imagery of washing the woman's feet would remarkably coincide with the message that she was washed clean of her sins. It would make for a great scene, and I imagine many sermons would be preached about it.

Yet that is not how the story goes. Jesus did not take dramatic action. Quite the contrary, Jesus allowed the woman to serve him. She started by washing his feet and pouring perfume on them—and Jesus just sat there. I think that by being present and allowing the woman to serve him, Jesus did something very significant. He gave the woman dignity—she washed the feet of *Jesus*. Few people can say that. What an incredible moment that must have been for her.

Served by Refugees

On one of my overnight visits to Mae La Refugee Camp on the Thai-Burma border, the Karen people shared more of their history. The Karen call the hills and jungles of Burma their home. They have lived in the jungles for generations—as far back as anyone can remember. So when the military dictatorship asked them to leave in order to access the valuable natural resources on their land, the Karen declined with steadfast will. They quickly became one of the most persecuted hill tribes for their resistance to give up their homeland and their way of life. After that, the military junta began systematically terrorizing them in what many human rights watchdogs affirm as crimes against humanity.

Soon after the refugee camp was settled nearly three decades ago, a Bible college began inside the camp. That the Bible college exists at all is amazing, let alone its reach in training Karen people from all along the Thai-Burma border.

Three of us spent the night in the camp in one of the bamboo huts attached to the Bible college. Frankly, we had nothing to offer the Karen people or the Bible college. As a lawyer I was practically useless in terms of skills that were readily applicable to the refugee situation. But no matter, we showed up and offered to help in any way we could. We brought our own food and water and came prepared to sleep on the floor. We did not want to be a burden—merely self-sufficient visitors. The Karen people have practically nothing, so we planned to ask nothing of them.

As soon as we set down our bags, three young Karen women came into our room. They brought beds with them consisting of a plywood sheet and four legs. We appreciated the gesture and decided raised platforms were better than sleeping on the floor. To our surprise, they returned with mattresses, then bedsheets, then mosquito nets. Coffee soon followed. Then, quite unexpectedly, they brought nearly endless amounts of food. And it kept coming—delicious Burmese food—the kind of ethnic cuisine that makes you wonder what you're eating, but tastes so good and so unlike anything you've ever eaten before that you want to savor every bite because you'll never find it at home.

We knew that refugee camps rationed food supplies, especially here. The camp administrators capped the number of refugees and capped the amount of food to match. Yet these administrative ceilings can't stop new refugees from flooding in every day. The people living in the camp won't turn away their brothers and sisters, so the rationed food gets rationed again and again. Rice is in short supply. Despite this, our Karen hosts continued bringing us food—more food than we could eat. We were stuffed at lunch—which we hoped was also dinner—but then even more food came late after dark. We attempted to eat everything, but our filled stomachs couldn't take any more.

We didn't ask for anything, but they delighted in making us happy. When you've been forced from your home, made to watch your village burn, are separated from family members, and are confined to a temporary camp without knowing what the future holds, I imagine it would be nice to know that you can still do something special for strangers. It would make you feel dignified.

Friend, lawyer. and "doer" Bob Goff shared a story from a school he founded in Uganda, the Restore Academy. Most students, who study farming on the academy's small garden plot, are on scholarship, sponsored by people from the United States. The students consume most of the food they grow, but one year a bumper crop presented the opportunity for the students to take vegetables down to the market for a lesson in commerce. The kids returned to the school quite proud to have earned a small amount of money. Bob suggested that they pool a portion of that money to sponsor an inner-city youth in the

United States. The Restore Academy students received youth profiles from an American nonprofit organization, chose a child to sponsor, and sent the money to the States.

Bob saw no reason for good acts to flow in only one direction—from the States to Africa. The Ugandan kids now have someone in whom they can invest. They know that they are making the world a better place while involved in a project that gives them dignity.

When I travel to some of the world's poorest places, I'm always amazed at how many people invite me into their homes. They want to feed me or give me water. I think it's universal human nature: when you get to do something for others—something that you truly want to do—it can be the greatest feeling in the world.

I think we all crave the feeling we get from doing something good for someone else. As good as it feels to help others, we need to turn the tables and allow others to do the same. We need to allow people to serve us, knowing they are making the world a better place.

Whatever We Can Bring

Like Michelle, I used to think I needed words or actions in order to help others. I'm reminded of my trip to Bangladesh, where I stayed far out in a village in the countryside. One evening at dusk I walked with my American companions through the center of town and happened upon a game of soccer. Naturally, the kids invited us to play, and we took them up on it. I was never a soccer kid, and I still can't play. But they let me play anyway and even passed me the ball quite often.

The village was a mixture of Bengali Hindu and Islam faiths. We were Christians from a different background and we couldn't speak their language. Some of us had soccer skills, some didn't. Some could converse, others couldn't. And many of us had very different worldviews. But what made it so great was that we brought all that we had to the field. And we had a blast. For some reason, we were heroes to them for playing, and the kids paraded us back the half-mile walk to where we were staying.

To the proverb of St. Francis of Assisi I might append, "Preach the Gospel at all times and when necessary use words *and actions*." "Go and do" starts with whatever we have to offer.

CHAPTER 11

Living Dangerously

ON MY TRIP TO BANGLADESH—the visit where I felt like I was an ambassador—the "go" part was not so easy. Truthfully, it was quite scary. I squirmed in my seat as the plane started its descent—my first time stepping out to go and do. The fasten seat belts bell chimed and the captain's voice came on over the PA system in a language I didn't understand. Nerves set in as the flight attendants secured the cabin. The Bengali man next to me could tell I was anxious. He struck up a conversation and asked why I would visit Bangladesh—it's not exactly a tourist destination.

My mental picture of Bangladesh was not one of safety and security. I recalled news footage from recent months of violent riots in the streets. I envisioned myself walking out of the airport and into throngs of angry people. But when the plane began descending, I realized there was no turning back.

Stepping out of the airport did not ease my trepidation. I walked into throngs of people—chaos, for sure, though not the angry mobs I had envisioned. I stood out as a foreigner, and everyone seemed to want something from me. They had a taxi; they wanted to carry my bags; they wanted to exchange money. And they gave me no personal space. The airport scene in Dhaka overwhelmed me and obliterated my comfort zone. This was my first trip to a developing nation alone—and, as of that date, the most dangerous country I had visited. Yet amid the madness outside the airport, I saw my name on a little white sign held by a driver.

Dhaka held more people in one small area than I could ever imagine. It was also the dirtiest, most poverty stricken place I had witnessed: people lay in the streets on top of piles of rotting garbage. The ride failed to calm my nerves. I held my breath when the police pulled our car over, furiously pointing at me, and yelled at the driver in a language I couldn't understand. What did I do, and what were they going to do to me? A few minutes later, they let us drive off in the other direction. Apparently Western-looking people can't drive past parliament on certain days. We definitely were not in the States anymore.

I felt as though I were watching myself in a movie. I pictured a camera crew following my taxi as we sped through the city, dodging in and out of heavy traffic, narrowly avoiding the occasional cow in the road. I felt like Indiana Jones—the life I had vividly, heroically imagined of myself over the last two years was actually coming true.

When the taxi finally arrived at my hotel, I ran inside. I locked and dead bolted my door, huddled up on my bed, and took a couple of deep breaths. I asked myself, once again, *What am I doing here?* Part of me wanted to catch the next flight back to safety. Another part was filled with the sensation that I was living on the edge.

Starting bright and early the next morning, I followed the Grameen Bank staff around Bangladesh as we visited rural villages exploring one of the world's poorest countries and this new, Nobel-Peace-Prize–winning-process called "microfinance." Little did I know that what would follow would be one of the most transformative weeks of my life.

On the last day, the bankers took me out for a few final interviews. My rickshaw pulled up to a small tin shed along what might be called this hamlet's "Main Street." I entered the dimly lit building to be engulfed by an earthy aroma and the drone of large motors.

I sat down at a small table with Shameen, the man who owned this business. He told me that a few years earlier, he and his family were very poor. Like many others, Shameen approached Grameen Bank for a tiny loan. The loan he received enabled his family to purchase grain and spice processing equipment. Now he owned a large building and employed nearly a dozen villagers. I arrived at the peak of harvest, and Shameen was busy.

Finished with his story, Shameen rose from his chair and motioned for me to follow toward one of the whirling motors. He stepped up onto a platform, reaching into a hopper above the machine. With both hands, he scooped up a handful of his raw goods to show me. The product? Mustard seeds.

The story from Matthew 17:20 instantly sprang to life: "If you had faith even as small as a mustard seed, you could say to this mountain, 'Move from here to there,' and it would move." I looked at Shameen and then at the multitudes gathering in the street. I thought about all the villagers' stories I had heard this week—like mustard seeds, these tiny stories about the life-changing effects of microfinance were moving the mountain of poverty.

Do What Scares You

Fear prevents a lot of people from ever getting to "go," often keeping people in the desert or not allowing them to come alive. In my work now, many students visit my office with a deep yearning to go and do something somewhere outside their comfort zones. But there's often trepidation in their voices. A common first question is, "Will I be safe?"

I believe that if something scares us, it's an indication that it might be the right thing to do. Fear often points us toward the things closest to Jesus' heart.

Consider the parable of the rich young man. He ran to Jesus and fell on his knees. He asked, "Teacher, what good deed must I do to have eternal life?" Jesus replied that if the man wanted to receive eternal life, he must obey the commandments. Rather than accept this answer, the young man kept prodding. "'I've obeyed all these commandments,' the young man replied. 'What else must I do?' Jesus told him, 'If you want to be perfect, go and sell all your possessions and give the money to the poor, and you will have treasure in heaven. Then come, follow me.' But when the young man heard this, he went away sad, for he had many possessions" (Matthew 19:16-22; see also Mark 10:17-22).

Jesus was not simply talking about wealth or giving; he was talking about fear. The rich young man's greatest fear was to lose his wealth, and that's what Jesus asked him to do. The rich young man could not handle the risk of giving up everything. He resisted sacrifice because he was afraid.

After the young man left, Peter asked about the disciples, who had given up everything to follow Jesus. Jesus replied,

"Everyone who has given up houses or brothers or sisters or father or mother or children or property, for my sake, will receive a hundred times as much in return and will inherit eternal life" (Matthew 19:29). Jesus identified the things that are hardest and most frightening to give up—safety, security, assets, and family.

Through the parable, Jesus urges us to assess our fears and ask ourselves whether they keep us from fully following God. If they do, then we need to confront those fears. Simply, we must embrace risk.

If we're moving toward God as we walk through our labyrinth, then we will encounter risk. For me, it was my pride—I feared my "go and do" experience might not rise to the level that met the traditional expectations of my profession. Was I willing to sacrifice that? Then there was also the risk of entering dangerous places and a fear of sacrificing cherished time at home.

Fear caused me to put more tension on the anchors where I was comfortable. And it drew me away from joy. If we can identify the things that scare us—the things we are hesitant to sacrifice—we might find that they point us in the direction of God and show us what it will take to go and do.

Lessons from Surfing

Surfers refer to something called the "stoke." You know when you're stoked; it's as if a fire inside you has been stoked to a flame. You will feel it on a big-swell day, when a large set of waves roll through. You see a wave coming, start paddling as hard as you can, and try to line it up. Your heart races as you "drop in" down the face of the wave. When you catch the wave, there's no other feeling like it. The "stoke" is a moment of pure joy.

When I think about fear pointing me toward the best things in life, I think about surfing. The bigger the wave, the better the ride and the better the rush—but also, the bigger the risk. When I get to surf larger waves, I often ride down the wave screaming because of the incomparable feeling. Yet waves can get exponentially heavier as they increase in size. A three- or four-foot wave might toss you around a little bit, but add another two to three feet in height and the wave can crush you like a rag doll.

Big-wave surfer Laird Hamilton is considered by many to be the best in the world at surfing giant waves. He pushes surfing to its limit, riding on waves that could easily take his life. I have no doubt that he gets scared.

Laird once wrote that when we stop taking risks, our bodies start to deteriorate. He is exactly right. I've seen many people deteriorate when they stop taking risks due to work, age, family, or, most often, fear. They lose strength, coordination, and the stoke—the joy.

The same principle of fear deteriorating our bodies applies equally to life and faith. If we fail to take risks, our lives deteriorate, especially our spiritual lives.

Though far from writing about the nature of God, author Anaïs Nin got it right when she wrote, "Life shrinks or expands in proportion to one's courage."[16] The courage to overcome our fears determines what our lives will look like—will they shrink or expand? Personally, I hope mine falls on the expanded side.

As pastor David Platt describes in his book *Radical: Taking Back Your Faith from the American Dream*, our vision of the gospel has become one of comfort and safety. The "American gospel" does not want to infringe on our security. It seeks prosperity; it avoids danger. But, Platt argues, we need to be drawn to uncertainty by the gospel. We need to risk it all.[17]

If we don't put a little risk into our spiritual lives, they can deteriorate quickly. The more we eliminate fear, the less we are forced to rely on God. Fear can strengthen our faith, especially if we're feeding it a relatively constant dose. It's like surfing increasingly larger waves, taking on things that scare you a little more every time. Then, when something big comes at you—the figurative big wave in your life—you're ready for it.

Fear Draws Us Closer to God

When we are afraid, we are forced to rely on God. My prayer life was the strongest and my prayer journal at its fullest during my first year of law school—especially my first semester with lousy midterms. Without a healthy dose of fear, we can get complacent, we forget to pray, and we rely on God less.

A few years ago, my friend Chad and I climbed Devils Tower in eastern Wyoming. Devils Tower stands as one of America's classic climbs—the core of an extinct volcano that rises eight hundred feet straight skyward. The Tower is an icon; the only protrusion sticking up above Wyoming's rolling plains.

Our climbing party of four included a guide and another climber named Jared. After climbing the first two pitches—a pitch being a two-hundred-foot rope length—we all huddled on a tiny ledge, barely big enough for the four of us to set up our next pitch. Looking down from this small ledge, I saw that the walls dropped straight off and, with the bluff that the Tower sits on, twelve hundred feet of air stood between us and the ground below. Our mortality became eminently and abruptly apparent.

As unexpectedly as Devils Tower appears on the flat plains of Wyoming, this question came from Jared: "So, why do you guys believe in God?"

Neither Jared nor our guide believed in God, and both quickly became quite vocal about it. Yet, in a situation where one wrong move meant certain death, something tugged at their souls. On that little ledge, assembling climbing anchors and organizing ropes, we discussed the existence of a supreme being. Looking down, Jared and our guide both wanted to believe in one.

I wonder if man's natural attraction to fear is actually a disguised attraction to God. Maybe many people, like our climbing companions, just don't realize it.

I believe I gravitate toward risk for this reason. I feel closer to God when I'm climbing or surfing. If our attraction to fear is actually an attraction to God, then it's no surprise that secular society is focused on safety.

Although I gravitate to risk, I feel haunted by the caution to "play it safe." As a society we create a pattern that "safer is always better." We enact stricter safety codes. We design life with blunt edges. I wonder if we're doing a disservice sometimes by removing the elements of fear and danger. Maybe we need to find a more healthy balance between fearless and fear less.

Consider what caution has done to our playgrounds. A few years ago I drove around to local parks looking for a merry-go-round or a teeter-totter. The park equipment I grew up playing on had all been replaced by colorful, fancy "play systems" that were all very, very safe. Nothing spun. There was nothing to fall off of. Everything was rounded, only inches off the ground, and equipped with extra guardrails. The playgrounds that I knew were the places where you learned what you were capable of—how many g-forces you could withstand or from what height you could survive a jump. Playgrounds were dangerous then, but there is little danger now.

I've read that more kids are being diagnosed with asthma, and doctors think there might be a link to the fact that they are playing inside more than before. Rather than being out in the elements and building immunity, they stay inside where there are fewer allergens. I'd hypothesize that we'd find the same link with fear. If we stay inside avoiding danger and living our heroic imaginations through video games, then we don't know how to test our fear in the real world.

I see this quite often in the way our students have been raised. When students say, "Well, my parents are nervous about my going to Africa," I get a good sense about whether or not they will take the risk of "going." Once the parents step in to plant the safe-playground philosophy into their kids' minds, the thrill of going quickly dies.

In reality, when our students make the decision to go, it's often more difficult for their parents. As Gary Haugen, founder and CEO of International Justice Mission, put it, "This is, of course, a tough step of faith for these young people, but it is a traumatizing leap of faith for their parents. For twenty-plus years these parents have been plowing the faith and love of Jesus into their children. And then shocking, their sons and daughters turn around and start acting as if it's all actually true. They simply go and do it! And their parents struggle."[18]

On at least one occasion I have received an angry phone call at my office from a parent—a parent of a graduate law student no less—because his or her child decided to "go" for the summer. Other students got cold feet because their parents e-mailed them daily news updates on the "dangers" in Africa.

As Gary Haugen wrote in his book *Just Courage*, kids ask why they've been given great education, structure, love, and discipline. Parents honestly answer, "So you'll be safe." The kids then ask, "Really? That's it? You want me to be safe? Your grand ambition for me is that nothing bad happens?" Haugen suggests that when they hear that, something inside them dies. They either perish in safety or they find adventure in the wrong places.

Learning to Live Dangerously

To a certain degree, fear can be helpful. Embracing risk does not suggest throwing caution to the wind and flying headlong into danger. Obviously, this can be a recipe for disaster and set the stage for the beginning of many bad situations.

Jesus' example in the desert cautions us against testing God with a "God will protect me" mentality.

Rather, we need to steadily and thoughtfully embrace risk. We need to teach ourselves daily to "live dangerously." Living dangerously isn't chasing large waves or putting ourselves in extreme danger; it's adopting a lifestyle that systematically overcomes the roadblocks we encounter. In a small way, I've adopted a guiding principle to help me seek out and overcome fear—I try to do one thing every day that scares me. Overcoming what scares me often becomes the most rewarding part of my day. Typically, it's something small. But these small things quickly build to bigger and deeper things. When you're faced with a question such as, "Do you want to go to Bangladesh?" or "Will you try outreach tonight?" then you're predisposed to say yes. When the time comes, being ready to say yes to those beacons of joy will lead to a more abundant, fulfilling life.

Surfer Laird Hamilton wrote about his own similar philosophy. "For those of us fortunate enough to live in places where our lives are relatively safe, I think if we challenged ourselves—even scared ourselves—once a day, we'd be better people. It helps to have that little jolt of perspective to remind you that life's fragile."[19] Scaring himself a little each day helps him prepare to tackle those big waves.

The things that scare us create the most important stories in our lives. In high school, I started to become afraid of heights. When I got to college, I took up rock climbing to combat that fear. Climbing has since taken me to some of the most amazing places on earth—like the top of Devils Tower. I can now walk up to the ledge of anything and look over. Height simply is not a big deal. More important, climbing is a significant narrative in my life. The climbs I've done composed some of my favorite stories and shaped my identity.

A handful of people have been born with unusually hard-wired brains that allow them to remember every single detail of every day of their lives. Scientists are studying them to learn more about how the brain and memory function. What the scientists are discovering is pointing them toward the importance of fear.

We remember times when we were afraid in great detail. I can recall scary moments as if they happened yesterday—car accidents, times I got in trouble, dinners where I had to eat fish, and a moment I almost drowned. I can picture the time of day, who was in the room, and what I was doing. I remember the surrounding conversations almost verbatim. Science is finding that the release of adrenaline does something to aid our memory. Adrenaline provides that daily jolt of perspective.

Fear builds our memories—the stories that make up our lives. Without fear, we'd remember much less and we'd be left with fewer stories to tell.

Embracing fear is one of the healthiest things we can do. As we embrace fear and learn to live dangerously, we will see life expand exponentially. We need that daily jolt of perspective. And as we discover those fears, we need to look closely and consider that perhaps fear is actually Jesus reminding us that life is fragile and that he wants to nudge us toward the things he cares about.

I fully believe that the best things in life are the things that scare me the most and make me the most uncomfortable.

When I was young, a story about Ethiopia caught my attention. A famine had struck the country. I remember watching television commercials depicting kids with bloated stomachs and flies on their faces. Even at age four, I wanted to do something about it. The TV probably showed adults in the images, too, but I only remember the kids. I remember the kids because I was a kid. I felt a bond to them. I was too young to have an understanding of the world of foreign policy or humanitarian aid. I was too young to have friends who could go there to help. I was too young to understand a famine or point to where Ethiopia fell on a map. Yet I felt somehow connected through the human experience.

Most of us don't know the fear of spending the night on the streets or not knowing when we will eat next. We don't know the desolation of not going to school because there are no schools. We don't know the trauma of being bought and sold as slaves. We don't know the abandonment of being thrown in jail with no advocate or redress. I certainly don't know any of those fears.

In the United States and most of the developed world, we live in relative affluence and comfort. We've sought the American Dream of owning a house and being financially secure. Most of the people I know and the students with whom I work haven't experienced severe pain—at least not the kind of deep pain where life hangs in the balance every day.

When we really look at the world, the fact that we live so comfortably can make us uncomfortable. We know that we have missed something that most of the world experiences. I find that those of us who haven't experienced much pain or hardship are actually drawn to it. When we know that other humans are suffering, we actually want to feel a bit of their pain because we wonder whether we could bear it too.

Years ago, someone I worked with on an anti–human-trafficking project told me she had not experienced much pain in her life—certainly not in comparison to the victims in our care. She believed that her lack of pain gave her the capacity to take on the pain of others. She felt that she had extra strength that she could use to yoke up with these victims and bear part of their burden.

There seems to be a mutual exchange in human suffering. Those of us who have not experienced suffering can offer our capacity to share the burden of those who are suffering. But those acquainted with suffering can also offer a great gift. For one thing, they remind us to appreciate what we have received and not to take our privilege for granted. They show us the fragile nature of humanity.

Nothing in life is scarier than the pain of human suffering. Even the most extreme adventures can't compare to the realities of the human condition. When we have little to fear in our own lives, we can shoulder the fear of others and challenge our own faith through their experience.

For those of us who have felt little pain, these harder edges of life remind us that what we have is real. They remind us that the people and opportunities in our lives are not fictitious—and they are not available to everyone. The raw human condition makes us appreciate what we have.

Most of all, loving those who really need it reminds us of our capacity to love. Showing up in Burma for Faifah—showing her that she's important—reminds me how much I can do with this capacity to love and that I have so much to go around. After trips to these places where I see the extremes of the human condition, I'm reminded of how to love other people. Though I venture to some of the grittiest places on earth, my trips are always a breath of fresh air. I return rejuvenated. I've conquered my fears and now I'm stronger—I'm equipped with stories to tell, and I've tested my faith. Fear has reoriented me toward God.

CHAPTER 12

Making Goodness Fashionable

WILLIAM WILBERFORCE is a hero of mine and of many others. Although he had the potential for significant upward mobility as a young British politician in the late 1700s and early 1800s, Wilberforce experienced his own "What am I doing here?" moment when he fell into his personal "Great Change"—a time when Wilberforce felt that God found him. Coming out of the "Great Change," Wilberforce found two things on his heart: the abolition of the slave trade and the reformation of morals. Wilberforce was appalled by the slave trade and worked tirelessly for years to see it abolished. Although it took his health and almost cost him his political career, Wilberforce succeeded in accomplishing this great task near the end of his life.

Summed up as his overall goal, Wilberforce "endeavored to make goodness fashionable."[20] Wilberforce wanted to change the hearts and minds of people and knew he was in a position to do so—to live a lifestyle of example.

In many ways goodness indeed became fashionable in Victorian England, thanks to William Wilberforce.

I wonder whether goodness is becoming "fashionable" once again. And I don't mean patting ourselves on the back for buying advocacy T-shirts or beaded necklaces made by victims of human trafficking, but focusing our energy instead on changed hearts and renewed minds.

A Space Race

On October 4, 1957, the Soviet Union launched the Sputnik 1 satellite. The Sputnik surprised the United States so much that then-president Dwight Eisenhower called it the "Sputnik Crisis." America was dumbfounded. Our nation thought we were leading the world in space exploration and technology, but the Soviet Union one-upped us. The "space race" had begun.

The heated space race soon grew beyond NASA and government research labs. New projects and programs rolled out across the United States, including an education program designed to advance America's children in math and sciences. We feared that if America's youth fell behind, the skilled intellect of Soviet engineers would surely surpass us.

This education program, labeled "New Math," speculated that the foundations for more complex mathematical ideas—such as set theory, functions, and abstract algebra—could be instilled in children at an early age. If children grasped these concepts, then math and engineering would significantly advance in the general population and, particularly, in future scientists.

Our personal revolution is our own Sputnik Crisis. The revolutionary spark sends our self-absorbed worldview a warning shot across the bow. We scramble to do something for ourselves that helps reconcile us with what we see in the world.

This crisis truly is a "space race." It's about mind space, those things with which we choose to occupy our thoughts and actions. Retailers figured out that our brains operate much like the shelves at a store. If you position your products and brands to occupy the most and best shelf space, that's what consumers buy. Brands and the companies behind them subsequently battle for retail shelf space. Advertising is all about "mind space"—those brands and products that get in front of us and occupy our thoughts.

In the case of our personal revolution, we can choose to give the human condition our attention or we can choose to ignore it.

Our old math focused on us. Like Aristotle and Ptolemy's geocentric model of the universe, where all planetary bodies revolved around the earth, the world seems to revolve around each of us.

But we live in an age of new math. The rules for the way we engage the world are torn apart—abstracted. We begin to make decisions based on what works and achieves the proper end, rather than being constrained by old formulas. The human condition begins to occupy our mind space and impact our choices. We accept greater responsibility toward others with our resources. We start adding things up differently.

The Price of a Latte

I like talking to Sama the Rastafarian, an undergraduate student who works for our Global Justice Program. "Sama," short for Samantha, is not really a Rastafarian. She's actually a follower of Jesus. I lightheartedly call her a closet Rastafarian because she changes the backgrounds on our computers to reggae themes and wears Bob Marley T-shirts to work at least twice a week.

Like many of her peers, Sama studied abroad. She spent a year in Argentina, then studied in Switzerland, traveling around South America and Europe. She wants to go to law school and practice criminal and human rights law. We sometimes discuss what she wants out of life and how her perspective has been shaped over the last few years of college and world travel. After the things she's seen and learned, Sama now summarizes her worldview like this: "I used to want a Rolex one day, but now I don't think I could ever justify it."

This is new math.

Like Sama, many who go and do start to rethink the way they spend money. Once people go and do, they begin perceiving life through the lens of comparison. Consider this: you could give up one latte every three days and support a child in Guatemala for a month. Or you could skip one meal per week and feed a child in Haiti for a month.

It comes back to mind space. I had lunch with a friend recently, and we talked about the idea of "consumerizing generosity." My friend once told me that he had walked into an upscale clothing store in Los Angles and saw a sign above one of the racks: "Buying This Shirt Might Save a Life."

We struggled to draw a connection between the purchase of a shirt and a human life. Maybe a percentage of the purchase would help fund an initiative somewhere in the world, but it seemed a bit of a leap. Someone had specifically designed the advertisement to reach the target audience, illustrating that we've become so conscious of "doing" and thinking so deeply in terms of this new math that it's now used as a sales pitch. My friend and I wondered whether this was a good thing. Did it make us more aware? The danger in this is that spending could replace "going" and consuming could replace "doing."

During graduate school, I lived in a dorm in Malibu,

California. When I graduated and dorms were no longer an option, Malibu suddenly became a much more expensive place to live; too expensive for me. I wish I still lived there—it's close to the ocean—but living there also messed with my mind space.

Malibu is a city of contrasts. Sometimes I would get coffee at a strip mall that had an exotic-car dealership, boutique clothing stores, and a restaurant where you could eat $100 Kobe beef from New Zealand. On weekends, this coffee shop became a destination for people to be seen with their Ferraris and Lamborghinis. I found it ironic that in order to get to this coffee shop, I had to pass an area on the side of the road where homeless men and women lived. They had built a little community in the bushes with blankets spread out and personal belongings hanging in the trees. Part of me always wanted to stop and walk down into that area. The contrast of the $300,000 Ferrari in front of me and the people living out of pilfered shopping carts intrigued me.

You have to look pretty hard to find these contrasts. Driving by, one might not even notice the bushes where the homeless live. Most of what you see in Malibu is affluence: giant homes on the ocean, estates in the mountains, and exotic cars. After a while, however, you become accustomed to it and think to yourself, *Hey, I deserve a Ferrari one day too.* I started thinking like this before my personal revolution brought me to new math.

I used to drive a nice car. I acquired it used right before I started law school. The previous owner had been in an accident, so it was priced reasonably. Some people say cars reflect who you are. If that's true, my car was probably a better representation of who I thought I wanted to become before I started law school. I thought graduate school would be a ticket to affluence and success. My personal revolution turned all of that upside down. After that, every time I walked to my car I was reminded that the person it represented was no longer who I wanted to be. At one place I worked, I parked down the street so that no one would see me driving it.

During the period of time in which I was struggling with my new math and who I thought I wanted to be, I flew home for a holiday. I sat on the plane next to a woman who couldn't fit into one seat and couldn't lower the armrest. For four hours I pushed my body as far into the opposite armrest as humanly possible. On this woman's left sat a squirrelly-looking guy with long, wispy hair. He wore a black Ewok T-shirt celebrating Star Wars. I put him in his early forties, but with the awkwardness of someone who lived his entire adult life in his mother's basement. As soon as he sat down, he immediately began talking to us about conspiracy theories—how the airlines pump jet fuel fumes into the cabin before takeoff to calm everyone down. I could not imagine a more horrible flight. I was dying. When I got off the airplane, I told my parents I would never fly economy class again. I was going to be a lawyer—lawyers don't fly economy. My parents just looked at me with blank stares—they weren't buying my tirade.

With my new math, however, I reconsider what conveniences are really worth the price. Economy or first class, either way gets me there. I might be more uncomfortable in economy, but I could put the money I would have spent on upgraded airfare to use for so many better purposes. I also imagine some of the refugees and victims of trafficking I know. I think about Faifah's two weeks in a crowded jail followed by her seven-hour ride in the back of a barbed-wire truck. I'm reminded of the imprisoned kids in Uganda who spent two years isolated on a cold, dark, cement floor. I know that if they can endure that, I have nothing to complain about on a twelve-hour flight.

I see nothing intrinsically wrong with owning a Ferrari or

flying first class. If you earned your money, you can spend it as you choose. I would love to own a Ferrari, and I would like to buy first-class tickets. But I know that the price of a $300,000 Ferrari could build a school and some dorms in Thailand. Upgrading to first class on a trip to Africa could fund a year of school for four or more kids in Uganda.

Learning to Give

My grandfather and I were discussing generosity and the value of contributing our time versus contributing our wealth. When the parable of the Good Samaritan came up, my grandfather looked at me and, quoting Margaret Thatcher, said, "No one would remember the Good Samaritan if he'd only had good intentions—he had money too."[21] I thought about that for a while. Margaret Thatcher might be right—we might not give so much praise to the Good Samaritan if he hadn't paid the hotel and medical bills of the wounded traveler. If we're serious about our good intentions, they can have a direct impact on the way we use our pocketbooks. If we are serious about "doing," then we must be serious about our new math. We must be serious about giving.

When we look out at the world and begin participating in this mutual rescue—a rescue where those we thought we came to help are actually rescuing us from our own despair—we realize how fortunate we are. I've often thought that it could just as easily have been me who was born on the street in Thailand or raised in a refugee camp. Once I understood that, I saw myself as less entitled to anything at all and more as a steward of significant resources.

Not only do we recognize that God asks us to give but also just how great an impact we can make with very little. For example, a twenty-five-dollar loan can, indeed, make the world a better place. Twenty-five dollars can provide the means for one of the poor to start a business—some chickens or a potter's wheel and clay—and from there, a whole new life.

I'm not good at being generous, but I am continually working on it and strengthening this act of obedience. I *want* to be generous, and every year I get a little better. I'm often convicted by 1 John 3:16-18. "We know what real love is because Jesus gave up his life for us. So we also ought to give up our lives for our brothers and sisters. If someone has enough money to live well and sees a brother or sister in need but shows no compassion—how can God's love be in that person? Dear children, let's not merely say that we love each other; let us show the truth by our actions."

It's easier for me to give what time I have than it is to open my pocketbook. This was especially true when I was a student. Yet I know that I'm asked to do both. And in many ways, I can be more helpful through the latter.

One of the hardest parts of giving is that we are bombarded by so many causes people want us to give to. At my grocery store, community groups frequently stand at the entrance asking for money. One day it's a youth sports club, the next day it's an LA drop-in center. If I see them there, I scurry past to avoid eye contact. Even on campus, it seems that there's constantly a student group raising funds for something. It starts to sound like static—to the point where we get "compassion fatigue." It's not that I don't believe these requests are important—they are—but I try to be intentional with my money, and when I'm confronted with a request that doesn't hit where my heart is leading, I don't know how to respond.

We underestimate the *me* part of generosity. We don't discuss it because it seems wrong to talk about yourself when you're giving. We are even told that we are not supposed to think about ourselves. Yet, we all do. We gravitate to our favorite charities and causes. When I think about myself, and find the places where I want my money to go, I find that I actually love to give. One of my favorite moments every year is when I get to donate to the kids I sponsor so they can attend school. It's a great feeling to go into the bank and make the transfer—to know that I am enabling kids I care about to get an education.

I love to give to these kids because they are important to me. The key is to discover what's important to you—what things make *you* come alive. You need to find something meaningful to you and invest in it. I really look at my commitment to the kids as an investment—I want to see long-term gain. I think in terms of five years, ten years, or even lifetimes, rather than moments.

When I work with our university fund-raising team, we run into two kinds of donors: those who accumulate wealth and give it all at the end of (or after) their lives and those who give as much as they can whenever they can, even though they might not have amassed huge bank accounts. I think I want to see my generosity at work while I am still alive. That feels more like an investment where I get some return. I want to participate in it. I want to be an actor, not an audience member.

At work we often quote George Pepperdine, the founder of the university, as saying, "What I had I lost; what I gave away, I still have." Beginning with a mere five dollars, George Pepperdine made a fortune by starting a car parts distributorship named Western Auto Supply Company. Pepperdine felt called to give his fortune away in order to help humanity. He envisioned an excellent Christian university and invested in that idea. Sometimes when I wander around campus, I think about what Pepperdine gave away and what he still has—an excellent university that still bears his name. It reminds me that what we give away now might grow into returns beyond our wildest imaginations.

The Future Looks Bright

New trends and movements often begin on college campuses. As I walk the Pepperdine campus, I get the feeling that goodness is, indeed, becoming fashionable—and in the best of ways. It's indoctrinated into the next generation at an early and impressionable stage.

In 1988 two students picked a day on the calendar and dedicated it to service. They repaired the homes of the elderly and planted a garden at a local elementary school. Giving a day caught on, growing into an annual event called "Step Forward Day" where fifteen hundred students and dozens of alumni chapters throughout the country now go into their local communities to serve nonprofits, schools, churches, and parks.

Farther from campus, hundreds of students every year give up the common spring-break party or trip for the chance to serve others in need. Known as "Project Serve," this movement sends students across the country and around the world on projects such as aiding inner-city schools in New York City or teaching English at orphanages in the Dominican Republic.

Many of the students I work with do amazing things that represent the best of what humanity has to offer. We celebrate their work as if "going and doing" is the highest of achievements. I know students who started a movement to identify slavery and human trafficking in downtown Los Angeles. Other students started a nationwide initiative called "Kind Campaign" to prevent bullying among girls—they even appeared on *The Oprah Winfrey Show*. Eighteen graduates this year committed to serving across the United States with Teach for America. Others went farther from home, moving to Kenya to build bread ovens for the rural poor or to Argentina to start microfinance programs for the destitute. A student-organized week highlighting Burma became a nationwide campaign and an organization called Lovemine.

One can't help but be inspired by their examples.

Now we can tell stories in ways that were unimaginable a few years ago. I started editing video in the mid-90s. I was in high school at that time, and the only reasonable method for editing involved recording between two VCRs. Then the computer-editing platform arrived in the late 90s, opening many doors toward professional quality and control.

Yet, not until the beginning of 2000 did video-editing technology become available to the mass consumer market. Now, high-quality digital video cameras come in our cell phones, nearly every laptop comes equipped with editing software, and we don't need even a single cable.

The video revolution exploded with YouTube. YouTube became a venue for storytelling like the modern-day version of the ancient Greek amphitheater. Video streaming has redefined the capabilites of the Internet.

However, video is not the only medium of information flow. Facebook boasts a clientele of over 800 million active users. Of these participants, half log into Facebook on any given day. Facebook estimates that the average user has 130 friends, connects to eighty objects of information, and creates ninety pieces of content each month. However, each video tells a story. Each Facebook profile tells a story. Each shared piece of content builds on these stories. Each status update deepens our stories. In short, we are overwhelmed by information, and we are bombarded by stories. The challenge now becomes breaking through the jungle of content to be one of the few that others connect with.

When I started making films, another filmmaker gave me a great piece of advice: it doesn't matter if you have bad footage as long as you have a good story. It's the "viral video" phenomenon—popular videos are viewed at an exponentially increasing rate because people want to share them. Viral videos become incredibly popular because they are stories worth sharing.

The Stories Jesus Wants Us to Tell

A master storyteller, Jesus told stories to teach the crowds who flocked to hear him and to preserve a message for future audiences who would one day read his words. Rather than give simple answers, Jesus taught in parables—short stories to convey his message and create reality. In many instances, he asked his listeners to place themselves in the shoes of the main character. In other cases, Jesus told stories through his actions.

Above all, Jesus' stories were not merely for entertainment purposes—the stories were commands to his audiences and examples after which to model one's life. In each of his stories, there was a takeaway—something meant to shape reality for us. To this, I ask, "What stories does Jesus want us to tell?"

Jesus wants us to seek out risk and danger. He wants us to hunt for challenges we must meet. At their end, our stories are about how we overcome those conflicts. Very few stories are shared where the protagonist fails. Jesus wants us to tell stories with our lives where we succeed. He points us toward conflict but gives us the tools to identify and overcome the obstacles we face.

Close to God's Heart

When we "go and do," we pursue the matters close to the heart of God, often authentically encountering God in the process. Thus, it's little wonder that the relationships forged through this process can be some of the strongest in our lives. "Going and doing" bonds people together at their deepest level. Pepperdine's Waves of Service movement grew from a request to organize and celebrate alumni service. Not only does the initiative allow the university and alumni to interact on a deeper level, but Waves of Service continues the vibrant "go and do" lifestyle after students walk across the stage at graduation.

This trickle-up, grassroots energy within the student body matches the university's mission statement and the vision cast by its leadership. The university culture now breeds students who "go and do" in beautiful synergy.

Other universities are adopting "go and do" cultures, as well. Belmont University gave its sophomore students up to twenty dollars each to "tell a better story" with their lives. Students had "twenty-one days to take the cash, pray, meditate, research, brainstorm and then use the money to make something happen in your life and the life of someone in need."[22] At Westmont College, students received twenty-five-dollar microfinance gift cards to donate to a borrower through Opportunity International and jump-start their interest in intentional giving.

During my first few years of law school, I heard about a movie that ignited college campuses across the United States. Three young film students, about my age, went to Sudan to make a documentary on the war taking place there. Unfortunately, they saw nothing to film. Heading home with nothing to show, the filmmakers ended up in neighboring Uganda, where they learned of the civil war led by the Lord's Resistance Army. There, they caught wind of a large group of children who walked to town every night to hide from the rebels. The rebels conscripted children through brutal techniques, forcing the kids to fight their dreadful war.

I borrowed the movie from the library, and the young woman at the circulation desk told me it had changed her life. The movie was titled, *Invisible Children*.

"Invisible Children" became their organization and movement. They loaded up vans, driving around the country to screen their film and tell the story. The movie stirred college campuses and churches, awakening the "go and do" virus in many people. Soon, Invisible Children built schools and dorms in Uganda to educate and rehabilitate the kids. Much of the funding for these Ugandan schools came from American schoolchildren. Invisible Children re-created the "night commute" across the United States as more than 80,000 people in 126 cities took to the streets to raise awareness for the children in Uganda in what became one of the largest demonstrations ever held for Africa.

Invisible Children is not the only organization inspiring action. For the last few years, I've been surprised to learn that the largest employer of Pepperdine college graduates is Teach for America. Teach for America was founded in 1990 by twenty-one-year-old Wendy Kopp, who envisioned the organization for her senior college thesis. She believed that her graduating peers desired to make a difference and would choose teaching over the more lucrative endeavors if the right opportunity existed.

Kopp was right. College graduates are turning down job offers and putting off graduate school to teach at public schools across the US, especially in urban and rural areas where the education system is in greatest need of motivated teachers. Why would graduates give it up to teach? Because they can "do" something. Teach for America corps members say they do it because they can see the difference in their students. And, a difference it has made.

If the elements for a personal revolution converge much earlier in life, the "go and do" lifestyle forms when a student is in high school or college. It alters career trajectories and goals— I witness it every day with students, and it brings great hope for what we might accomplish. I know I'm spending time with people who will live lives of generosity and change the world— people who will rescue victims from trafficking, will feed the hungry, and will breathe inspiration into another generation. And this group is young—they won't tell one good story, but many throughout their lives. It's a future worth getting excited about.

A Tennis Lesson

I once read an intriguing interview of Andre Agassi conducted by a young tennis pro. Sitting next to Agassi on an airplane, the young pro asked him a question: what is your biggest regret? Agassi's answer didn't involve a botched backhand, something he confessed in his memoir, or any tennis moment, for that matter. Agassi immediately responded that he regretted not starting his nonprofit organization earlier. His highly regarded organization now serves many children with disabilities, and he actively participates in the work. Agassi is extremely generous, and he gets to witness the fruits of his labor.

I really resonated with Agassi's answer. My small nonprofit doesn't do grand things like his does. But I love it. I like doing the little bit that I can with the little bit that I have. I'm glad I didn't wait.

CHAPTER 13

All the World's a Stage

"I DON'T UNDERSTAND why you go overseas, when so many problems exist here in America," a woman in a blue polo shirt protested.

I sometimes visit local graduate school fairs to recruit for Pepperdine. I stand by a little table to answer questions about law school and our Global Justice Program. At one such event, a staff member from another school approached me.

She was recruiting for another university's social work program. Taken aback by the confrontation, I realized that I had never sufficiently thought this through, and as a result, was unable to offer an immediate, well-reasoned, and succinct answer. It had seemed natural to respond to people in need no matter where they lived. I never found it strange that this might require flying over some oceans to do so.

Reflecting later on the woman's statement, I realized that I never divided need by continent. And I still don't. I don't see a difference between serving those at home and serving those abroad. I entered life at a time when global politics were changing and technology was booming. Consequently, I think I see the entire world as an opportunity. This lens seems natural to me, but I recognize that it might not be so immediate for those who grew up in a different time. Nonetheless, we're all realizing how globally connected we really are.

My sister, Eliza, is a seminary student. I brought her with me to Thailand on one trip, and we again stayed at Mae La Refugee Camp with the Karen people. She walked away from the experience with that "coming alive" feeling. When she returned to seminary in Minnesota, she was able to attend a Karen church service because the state of Minnesota has resettled a large portion of the Karen population. Eliza asked at the church if she could get involved and was directed to a recently resettled Karen family.

Arriving at the apartment at the predetermined time, Eliza took a deep breath and knocked. There was no sound in response. She could hear the chatter of the Karen language coming from other rooms down the hallway, so she knew she was in the right building. But from that room there was nothing but silence. She stood there awhile, wondering if she had mistaken the date or maybe the apartment number. Finally, a man came down the hallway and walked toward this apartment, so she explained that a woman from the church had set up this time for her to work with him and his family on English.

The man only smiled and nodded. Entering his apartment, he left Eliza at the open door. Was she supposed to go in or wait patiently outside until the rest of the family showed up? He kept looking at her and she kept looking at him, until finally he made some gestures that suggested she should enter the apartment to wait.

The man mumbled things in Karen and smiled politely while Eliza tried to ask him once more about the woman from church. He handed her a letter. Thinking he wanted her to help him sort through the mail, she asked if he had any other mail that they could sort. He said yes and politely smiled—but he made no move. Then it dawned on her—the man had no idea what Eliza was saying. He was so polite that it took a while for her to realize that not only did he not understand what she was saying, but he also had not been expecting her; he had no idea what she was doing there. He had just kindly invited her in.

Eventually he walked out of the room, leaving Eliza to sit silently on the couch and debate whether to stay or go. Finally he brought in an eight-year-old Karen girl who walked up to Eliza and spoke perfect English. At last Eliza was able to tell him she had come to help with English. As she told me, "He pulled out his English lesson books to show me what he was studying. He flipped to a specific page and pointed to the words his teacher said he needed to learn. Did it start with 'Hello' or 'How are you'? No. The first English word this man had to learn: 'Priority Mail.' I kid you not."

Eliza learned that the man was hoping for daily tutoring, and she agreed to return as often as her schedule allowed. As she explained, "With that our lesson came to an end. I didn't teach him a thing—and he certainly didn't learn to say 'Priority Mail.' But as I walked out the door, the eight-year-old girl noticed my Karen bag and asked how I had obtained it. I told her about my trip to Thailand and my stay with the Karen people at the Mae La refugee camp. She was delighted to hear it—she had lived at Mae La before moving to Minnesota. I pulled a few pictures out of my bag to show them both my stay at the camp. Then, before I could move out the door, the man asked me to wait. He brought forth a traditional knitted Karen shirt and handed it to me. The girl explained it was for me to have as a thank-you. I was taken aback—I certainly hadn't done anything that deserved a gift. But that gesture reminded me of the generosity of the Karen people and how thankful people can be when we are willing to step out."

Eliza's story blurs global boundaries. We still think in terms of continents and borders, but there are international needs right in our own backyard.

Where Once There Were Borders

I've founded my own nonprofit, I've started for-profit businesses, and I've been a part of dozens of early start-ups—some of which became realities and some of which never made it further than the napkins upon which they were sketched. I believe the hardest part in any early organization involves choosing the name. Everyone's got an opinion, and when you finally find the perfect expression, someone's already purchased the ".com" or ".org."

When I think about names for organizations, I find one naming practice particularly intriguing: "[fill in the blank] Without Borders." It seems like there's a "_____ Without Borders" for everything. "Doctors Without Borders" is the classic—the organization does exceptional medical work in places of great need. There's a "Lawyers Without Borders," "Teachers Without Borders," and "Engineers Without Borders." These all make sense to me; I can picture what they do.

Others are more esoteric. "Action Without Borders" and "Words Without Borders" strike me as particularly mysterious. Finally, some are downright amusing: "Geeks Without Borders," "Bikers Without Borders," and my favorite, "Clowns Without

Borders." I wouldn't name my organization "_____ Without Borders," not because I think there are too many organizations with that nomenclature and it's lost its novelty (I do think this), but because I think the name is now conceptually irrelevant. Simply put, borders for the most part don't exist anymore.

Few true borders still survive anywhere in the world. Many fell with the collapse of the Iron Curtain and the end of the Cold War, and those that are left are quickly fading. If you get the chance, visit a true border before they completely disappear. While you're at it, take a picture there to show your grandchildren.

The demilitarized zone on the border between North Korea and South Korea is one of the few true borders still remaining. It may be the last place in the world where the West and the East still bump against each other, sometimes colliding in heated standoffs. I would not be surprised to wake up tomorrow to learn that North Korea had collapsed and refugees from North Korea were flooding into South Korea. At that moment one of our last borders would be gone, marking the end of an era.

Although we are becoming more interconnected and streamlined, the novelties that represent borders are fading along with them. I enjoy opening official envelopes from embassies, pulling out my passport, and thumbing through the pages in search of a colorful new visa. I like the tension of crossing a border into a new country. I experience some kind of strange rush when I hear the sound of the stamp hitting my passport. I walk across a border into a new country, and I celebrate the fact that I'm allowed to enter.

In many ways that was yesterday's process. Today I can take a train around Europe and get waved through as I cross between European Union member countries. Some of the countries I travel to in Africa no longer require visas.

As the concept of the border disappears, likewise our own worldview needs to shift from nationcentric to global. The result is that our lexicon for describing global need will move from a detached "there" to a collective "here."

Have You Ever Used a Pay Phone?

Recently, in the Denver International Airport I had a moment of unique self-realization. Flying from California to South Dakota via Colorado, I stepped onto the moving walkway between gates. I took a call from the West Coast of the United States while at the same time reading e-mails from Rwanda and India and text messages from Thailand. That moment put me in awe of how small the world seemed. I marveled at what I couldn't comprehend, such as the Internet, for starters. I've read that the Internet moves in tiny packets of data. I can't wrap my mind around how little clumps of 1s and 0s are encoded and then decoded to make messages and images. For that matter, I can't comprehend the workings of telecommunications, jet engines, and even moving walkways—all technologies I was using at the moment.

One of the experiences I'm most thankful for is that I experienced life before much of this recent globalization happened. At about five years old, I remember going shopping for Christmas. We often shopped at a store in town called Best, a precursor of sorts to the big-box stores of today. It stood as a large, windowless building separated from the mall. The inside resembled a warehouse, with an unfinished interior. The store had a showroom where you picked out what you wanted and asked a store clerk to retrieve it for you. Sometimes larger items stored in the back would roll out on a metal conveyor belt made of hundreds of tiny metal wheels. If we wanted stereos, TVs, or appliances, we found it at Best. This store, and the few others in town, formed our entire world when it came to shopping. If other products existed anywhere—better products—we didn't know about them. It seemed adequate at the time, but now when I reflect on those days, I am reminded of the stories of settlers shopping at the general store in their prairie town.

Sometimes Best wouldn't stock what we were looking for, so we would call home to ask my mom for her input on the purchase. Two pay phones stood near the entrance to Best, and I still remember inserting quarters into them. I didn't see a cell phone until quite a few years later. It was my neighbor's, and it came attached by a cord to a large duffel bag, almost like a briefcase.

Memories of shopping at Best and using pay phones help me appreciate that we have cell phones and the Internet today. I don't know where I would even find a pay phone anymore—many have been removed. I also rarely purchase anything in brick-and-mortar stores now. I do most of my shopping online so that I can review everything available and find exactly what I want. For that matter, I've even shopped the Internet from my cell phone while riding a moving walkway in the airport.

These memories for current generations will slowly fade and eventually become nonexistent. The youngest members of our generation may never see the world the way it was. (And, I must admit, even I am still a little shocked when grade school kids have their own cell phones.) It's harder to appreciate what we have when we don't know where we came from.

During my time in Bangladesh, I saw that the rest of the world is not lagging. If anything, it moves faster than those of us in the said "developed world." Bangladesh jumped right over landline phones. I'd be surprised to find a phone booth in the country at all. The phone line infrastructure simply doesn't

exist, and the task of connecting every house seemed too daunting. Instead, Bangladesh went straight to wireless, putting up
mobile phone towers throughout the country.

In 1997 Grameen Bank created the concept of "telephone
ladies," which took off and proliferated the mobile phone.
Phone ladies are, essentially, walking pay phones. The ladies
purchase cell phones and airtime minutes with their microloans,
and then they sell phone calls to the villagers. This changed
Bangladesh. Prior to this, if Bengali villagers wanted to ask a
relative or doctor a question, they might have to catch a rickshaw, then a bus, and maybe a cab to cross even a small portion
of the country. It could take days and it would be expensive—
weeks or months of income. But now they can make a phone
call for a fraction of a day's wages.

At first, phone ladies became the wealthiest people in the
village. But soon their business model fell through the floor.
Mass-produced cell phones became extremely cheap, and airtime minutes joined the cost-effective ride—cell phones became
economical enough for nearly everyone to afford. I was stunned
to find in one rural village that most people possessed a cell
phone. I even photographed the locals taking photos of me
with their camera phones. At the time, my cell phone in the
States didn't even have a built-in camera. The rural Bengalis
were ahead of *me* in technology.

I wondered whether the Western world could be completely
overtaken in technology. Bangladesh doesn't have any moving
walkways—at least none that I saw. Maybe they're just waiting
for teleporting technology to become available. Despite who
may be implementing the latest technology quickest, we cannot
underestimate how it is reshaping our lives and our borders. It's
allowing us to be at all places at all times, and it's shortening the
distance between any two people.

The Overview Effect

The most widely distributed image in history might be The Blue Marble. The beautiful, iconic imagery of The Blue Marble portrays Earth hanging in the blackness of space, the first clear picture to show Earth in its entirety. Photographed by the crew of Apollo 17 on December 7, 1972, the photo was taken on the last manned lunar mission, the last opportunity for humans to be in the range where a photo of the whole Earth is possible. The astronauts thought Earth looked like a marble, with its swirls of blue and white.

Many of our early astronaut heroes possessed a deep faith in God. Some even found God during their flights, swinging around the moon to see their first glimpse of Earth as they descended back into the atmosphere. I imagine them looking at the The Blue Marble in real life and feeling completely overwhelmed. As John Glenn, the first American to orbit the Earth, marveled, "To look out at this kind of creation and not believe in God is to me impossible."[23]

The astronauts felt a profound sense of universal connectedness as they viewed Earth from space, which became a documented experience termed "The Overview Effect." Rusty Schweickart, an astronaut on Apollo 9, experienced it on a space walk in 1969. "When you go around the Earth in an hour and a half, you begin to recognize that your identity is with that whole thing. That makes a change. . . . It comes through to you so powerfully that you're the sensing element for Man."[24] Schweickart sensed the interconnectedness of humanity.

While few of us may ever go into space, I believe their experience isn't that far removed from what we experience when we "go and do." Schweickart spoke of traveling around the Earth in an hour and a half—and I resonate with that. I felt like I had circumnavigated the globe from my cell phone in Denver International Airport. From an international airport, I can board a plane, fall asleep, and wake up practically anywhere on the planet I choose. Faifah can call someone in Thailand, who calls me. I buy a plane ticket and see her nearly twenty-four hours later. You begin to recognize your identity is with the whole thing.

When we "go and do," we experience a version of the Overview Effect without going into high-Earth orbit. Technology and a borderless world give us the spacelike perspective with our feet still firmly planted on terra firma. At that moment, we realize how small the world seems and how many people call this one, tiny marble in space home. At that moment, as the astronauts discovered, faith takes on a new meaning. We want to tell the world where we've been and what we've seen.

The woman in the blue polo shirt who had confronted me had not yet had an Overview Effect experience of her own, though I suspect she will eventually. We're all in it together. Some of us commute downtown to "go and do," while others commute across oceans. We all serve the same humanity before the same God. The world is, indeed, our stage.

CHAPTER 14

Putting It All Together

"WHEN ARE YOU going to come to Uganda?" I pinned this question on Jim the Professor outside his office door. I sidestepped into his path to corner him.

"You're never going to get me to Africa," Jim responded quickly, dodging my attempted blockade as he darted down the hallway.

"I dare you to come with me!" I shouted at his back, raising the stakes.

Without breaking stride, Jim turned his head, smirked, and retorted, "I don't think so." He flapped his hand as if to wave me off like an unrelenting magazine scam.

Jim the Professor has a wife, three kids, and a little dog with a pink leash that he's not very fond of. He convinced his family to name the dog "Janie" after Aerosmith's song "Janie's Got a

Gun" to give himself a sense of justice against the tiny animal.
Jim the Professor served as the associate dean of student life and
teaches tort law—the kind of law that might be useful if someone takes out your eye with a bottle rocket or spills hot coffee
on your lap. He used to work for a prestigious American firm,
where he was on track to becoming partner. Yet he gave it all up
because he wanted to teach law and be a part of building a top
law school. He felt a yearning to "go and do" in a community he
loved and returned to his law school alma mater. Jim is someone
who always has his office door open to students to laugh with
them, to pray with them, and to cry with them. And students
know it—they flood his office. They also know that if they have
struggles in their lives, Jim will fight passionately for them.

When I first got to know Jim, he didn't seem interested
in global outreach. If he had the opportunity to be out of the
office, he might prefer to take his family to Disneyland, a zoo,
or somewhere equally safe. Yet I kept inviting him to join me,
partially because I hoped he might crack and partially because I
amused myself watching his expressions as he told me no.

Jim would admit that God—not just my good-natured guilt
tripping—started working on him. Though he came from a
past legal career to "go and do" among the Pepperdine community, Jim's heart had not yet been captured to "go and do"
beyond America. He began regularly attending Global Justice
Program events. I'd see him standing in the back of the room.
Jim attended the events where our students shared their "go and
do" stories from places like Uganda, Rwanda, and Thailand. He
also crossed paths with most of those students on matters that
involved his role as dean of student life.

A few months later Jim and I attended a conference of
Christian lawyers. Bob Goff happened to be a speaker and
gripped the audience with his message of "leaking Jesus." Bob

told stories about his own work in Uganda, following Jesus, and doing justice. I sat a few seats away from Jim the Professor. Every once in a while when Bob said something particularly useful, I'd look over my shoulder and stare at Jim. He looked uncomfortable, squirming in his seat and wearing an expression as if he had something heavy on his mind. After the session I approached Jim immediately.

Before I could say anything, Jim spoke.

"Okay, I have to go," he confessed, wearing an I-just-received-bad-news facial expression.

"Where?" Maybe he felt sick and needed to go back to his room.

"I have to go to Africa," Jim replied. "I know I have to go."

"Are you serious?" I asked, a bit bewildered. "Let's make it happen then."

Just Go

On a previous trip to Uganda, I had visited the country's largest prison and spent time in the "remand" area. Remand is the period between the time when the accused are arrested and when they stand trial. Unfortunately, sometimes they wait for a very long time because of case backlog. Remand presents a more daunting problem for children, especially children who live out of the city in the bush. It can be easy to slip through the cracks when you don't have a voice. We got word of a "remand home" for children in central Uganda where kids sit as long as two years without trial. Bob Goff, who also teaches for our Global Justice Program, suggested that we could show up and build their cases. The idea sounded great in the abstract, but we didn't know exactly whom to call or how to get it set up from the States.

"Let's just book the tickets," I argued. Jim was on board

for the trip, and now we needed to get something set in stone. With our intended time frame for arriving in Uganda now only a few weeks away, our window of opportunity to organize a trip seemed to be closing. "I know that we aren't sure what's going to happen, but I think we might have to just go there and figure it out," I said.

My "just go" suggestion didn't comfort Jim. Our original plan looked great on paper, but as they say, the best laid plans of mice and men often go awry. And go awry it did. We struggled to reach the necessary clerk of courts in Uganda to secure the files. By the time we finally did reach her, the court clerk wasn't sure she could get the files. We couldn't get definitive answers from anyone. On top of that, airfare increased rapidly with violent, daily swings. Compounding our problems, two alumni hoped to join us, and we feared planning something that didn't materialize would waste their time and money too. Everything seemed to work against us.

When you "go" to a place that faces immense challenges, you don't know what will happen until you get on the ground and march into someone's office. Even then you expect most things not to go as planned. Instead, you need to roll with it. In our eleventh hour, with the trip on the chopping block, we took the leap of faith and ordered the tickets.

Tickets in hand, David the Environmentalist and Ray the Litigator rounded out our four-man trip. David the Environmentalist isn't an environmentalist in the tree-hugging, Prius-driving sense. He's a family man like Jim, and he started an environmental law department at a major utility company. He works from the inside out to make utility companies more environmentally responsible. Ray the Litigator knows his way around a courtroom, winning large cases. He's good at it too: he helped secure a $600 million settlement in a series of child abuse cases. Ray booked his flights mere days before departing. His constantly fluctuating court schedule can make advance planning a challenge. Up until we saw him at the airport, we weren't sure whether he would even be on the flight.

Arriving in Uganda, we immediately started out on our hour-plus drive from the airport. I turned around from the front seat of the taxi to watch their expressions. Everyone looked like deer in headlights. Jaws dropped in a combination of jet lag and mild terror. Brief panic ensued with each close call on the road. Between the masses of people everywhere, traffic in chaos, and shops along the road selling indiscernible vegetables, the drive would be a nightmare for anyone with attention deficit disorder. Life in Uganda is raw.

I asked Jim the next morning for his first impressions. "I don't know," he replied. "I thought I was going to fall in love with Uganda, but . . . well, I don't think I would ever bring my wife here."

We hired a car and started the long drive to Gulu, Uganda, in the north.

Gulu marked ground zero for the war between the Ugandan army and the rebels in the bush. Rebel leader Joseph Kony and his followers, the so-called Lord's Resistance Army, notoriously destroyed villages, forcibly conscripted young boys into their army, raped women and girls in their way, and set thousands of land mines throughout the north. While fighting carried on from the mid-1980s through the early-2000s, the government created displaced persons camps and herded Uganda's northern inhabitants into those sites, ostensibly for their protection from the rebels. Now that the war is over, their land is lost and the people possess few skills for sustaining themselves.

We headed to Gulu to visit one of these camps that once housed thirty thousand people. Upon our arrival, children appeared from everywhere. Born at the camp and quickly orphaned by war and the AIDS epidemic, the kids wore tattered clothing, possessed virtually no food, received little schooling, and had even less hope of a brighter future. The leader of the camp took us on a walking tour while the kids jockeyed to hold our hands.

One girl stood out. She wore a bright pink dress. Her head was shaved to keep cool in the warm temperatures, but she was beautiful. Her eyes were wide and bright, her smile large and beaming. She held David's hand the entire time we were at the camp. She spoke English, and David learned that she was the same age as his own daughter.

Sometimes we're drawn to people through an undeniable, inexplicable connection. I had felt that kind of deep, God-arranged connection to Song, Noi, and Faifah in Thailand. You just know that there's a reason you met. David seemed to feel the same about this girl. I don't know whether he saw his own daughter in her or she stole his heart with her smile, but it was something deep and mysterious in the realm of things God arranges. David continued talking about the girl in the pink dress for the rest of the week.

The Masindi Project

Our quest to serve the children in prison took us to a small, sleepy town in Uganda's bush and a gateway city to the notorious north. Despite being only a few hours out of the relatively modern capital of Kampala, little seems to have changed since the days of the early explorers. Modern comforts have gained little foothold: rural, subsistence living remains the mainstay. Our hotel proudly celebrated that Ernest Hemingway had stayed there—even naming the bar after him. One might expect to find the writer still roaming the streets. Life seems to have changed little since his time, and the town still reflects the Africa of his stories.

In many ways we, too, were explorers—not the geographical type, but explorers discovering the fringes of the rule of law. Like the untamed wilds of the bush, traditional notions of justice often find their resolution through mob justice—violent, groupthink acts of revenge. Few Ugandan justices or lawyers desire to serve this region. Only the hearty and humble accept such posts. Not surprising, access to justice proved no easy task for anyone, especially children. We journeyed largely into the unknown—unsure of what to expect, not knowing whether we could actually be useful.

Our first day in Masindi took us immediately to the local courthouse to meet with the magistrate judge. Upon arrival, we learned that the judge had received a letter from the head of all the trial courts in Uganda telling him that we were coming and that he should help us. Unfortunately, the letter said we would be arriving two days later than our actual arrival, so none of the files were ready. The only initial information we could pull together about the children's cases was their names and the crimes they were accused of committing: murders, rape, kidnapping, weapons possession, and theft.

The kids, ages thirteen to seventeen, waited in a "remand home." After juveniles are arrested in Uganda, it can take several days or even months before they are charged with a crime. During this time they are sent to the remand home to await their trial.

We drove out of Masindi and onto a bumpy dirt road requiring a four-wheel drive vehicle. The red clay trail snaked out of town, up a hill, and into the bush. Fifteen minutes later a left hook brought a series of small mortar buildings into view. The buildings showed their age, as if they had seen better days. The walls were weathered, with large cracks and missing chunks of plaster exposing the red bricks underneath. A cursory glance might lead one to think this was a small farm. A farmhouse, barn, and stable stood on the property, with two large gardens completing the picture.

Our 4x4 pulled under the shade of a large tree. A few children and uniformed adults emerged from the buildings, warily glancing to see the foreigners. David, Jim, Ray, and I began walking slowly toward the buildings, proceeding with trepidation despite being accompanied by the judge and the warden.

The main building before us stood formidable and imposing: tall, blank, beige walls and a broad, single-point roof. The windowless prison allowed air flow for only a few iron-rod passages near the convergence of wall and roof. The facade was simple—a large wooden door with a large padlock. Obviously the builder wanted to prevent anyone from entering or exiting. Etched above the door was the year of the building's birth: 1962.

In the middle of the door, a small square hole was cut into the thick wood in order to pass items in and out. The inky blackness inside told us there was no light entering the room, even during midday. Soon, a youthful face emerged from the darkened opening. The outline of his face and the whites of his eyes reflected dashes of light from outside. The face disappeared as the warden stepped away from our group and approached the door. He undid the padlock, and the door opened. We followed.

As I stepped through the doorway, my eyes took a moment to adjust to the change in light. The stale air felt cool and heavy, but almost made me gag with the smell of must. We entered unprepared for what we saw. Eighteen boys lined the walls and shared no more than a dozen mats—mats made of reeds covered with old bedsheets. Coated with hieroglyphic-like etchings, the walls archived the names of current and past residents, messages, and phone numbers. This prison obviously had housed many residents over the years. The boys sat in the front half of the cell—the floor on the back half flooded with water from a small room resembling a restroom.

In a local dialect, the judge and warden told the kids that we were lawyers from America and that they needed to answer the questions we asked. The judge then asked which of them spoke English. Only two raised their hands. Both became our interpreters. The warden sent the boys outside to fetch plastic chairs from a neighboring building. After the introduction, we walked outside to gather underneath a large tree where we would set up for the interviews and meet the three girls at the facility. The girls lived in a separate, smaller shed turned jail cell.

Africa used to be known as "the dark continent" because nineteenth-century mapmakers knew so little about Africa's interior that they would color the large, blank void with dark ink. Though today the reference is controversial, many of us are still a bit like nineteenth-century mapmakers. That is, we choose to leave places dark in our minds and hearts because we're not willing to go see what's there. From under the tree I looked out over the rolling bush of Africa and marveled at our smallness. Here we sat, the four of us in the middle of nowhere on this giant continent. We were way off the grid—somewhere in the dark spaces on those old maps.

Interviewing the kids brought challenges at first; the children spoke softly and avoided eye contact. It was clear that these kids, with the exception of our interpreters and a few of the recent arrivals, were broken, defeated, and lacking hope. We soon discovered that our interpreters were brothers accused of murder. They had been in the remand home for two years awaiting a hearing. Yet despite their awful circumstances, they were polite, pleasant, and intelligent.

David and Jim began interviewing Henry, one of our interpreters. Henry stood tall, and his slender, athletic build made him look suited to run marathons. He spoke politely and decidedly, as if he served as a spokesperson for the entire crop of boys. His poise and intellect reflected a future leader rather than a hardened criminal. We learned that the prison operated under its own homegrown governance. The boys had elected Henry the leader. He watched out for them, represented their interests to the warden, and even taught informal elementary classes.

We learned that Henry, his brother Joseph, and their father were accused of beating a man to death. The man had worked for Henry's father as a herdsman for two days before stealing $115 from under their father's mattress. A mob of angry villagers murdered the accused thief the next morning. Henry and Joseph heard the commotion from school. When they returned home that afternoon, a jealous neighbor used the opportunity to call the police and accuse the family of murder.

Unfortunately, this was not the only case against Henry. A few months prior to our coming, a new boy had arrived at the remand home. Every afternoon prison guards took all the boys out into the field to grow and gather vegetables. The new boy did not cooperate. While working in the fields, he suddenly took off running. The prison guards sent Henry and some of the other boys after him. The prison guard forced Henry, the leader of the boys, to administer corporal punishment—a spanking with a branch—as an act of authority and to set an example. The boy was then asked to sit by the tree. He complained of not feeling well, so he was released to return to the remand building and wait for the rest of the boys to return.

When the fieldwork was finished, the young boy was found dead in the remand home.

The prison guard was accused of murder and so was Henry. Some of the boys testified that the victim often struggled to breathe—he had asthma. All in all, the purported injuries didn't add up to the death. Our working theory was that the boy returned to the remand home, where he suffered an asthma attack. Henry had acted at the behest of the guard, we suggested, and his actions did not cause the death. We were convinced he should not be charged with murder.

The next day, I tried to go to the public prosecutor's office— the governmental department bringing the murder charge against Henry and the other cases against the boys. I wanted to review as many files as I could. We waited. The prosecutor had made himself "unavailable" to us all day. Then, with only a few minutes before the office closed, he let us inside. With only fifteen minutes I couldn't do much and I couldn't take the file. Oftentimes, the defense in Uganda doesn't get to see the file until trial. Thus, they don't know all the evidence in it. What I might learn here could solve the case, I hoped. I blasted through as many files as I could see—speed reading for key terms—then, finally, I came to my last file: Henry's second case.

Henry's second case looked to be an inch thick. It had so many documents and police reports and notes that I couldn't make sense of most of it. Only a few minutes left now, and we would be kicked out. I scrambled through the papers for anything that might jump out. Then I came across the header, "Autopsy Report." This was what I had been looking for. The examining doctor wrote about various bruises from the spanking. At the bottom, he had scrawled, "Injuries do not explain cause of death." I'd seen movies and TV shows where lawyers find a single, hidden piece of evidence that changes the whole case, and this was it. This was our proof that the boy's death was independent of Henry's actions. It supported our asthma theory.

Later in our week we paid for Henry and Joseph's mother to travel to Masindi for an interview and to see her sons. She verified that the boys were in school at the time of the crime, and we called the headmaster to corroborate. Their mother told us that the boys attended special school on scholarship from the government because of their intelligence. If they were verifiably in school, then they couldn't simultaneously be at the scene of the crime. We were convinced that the evidence proved their innocence.

The second day of interviews brought us further heartbreaking stories. One of the three girls, Scovia, told us of her murder charge. She had turned seventeen on Christmas Day, three months after her two-week-old baby died. After Scovia became pregnant, the baby's father left to serve in Iraq with a private security company. She went to live with her alcoholic grandmother, who didn't want her but tolerated Scovia's presence as she prepared to give birth. Shortly after the baby arrived, he became sick and vomited continuously. Scovia asked her grandmother for money to go to the hospital, but the grandmother told her this was normal. While the grandmother left on a drinking binge, the baby passed away. When the grandmother returned, she refused to let Scovia bury the baby on the land, believing that evil spirits would accompany such a burial. Mourning her loss and not knowing what to do, Scovia wrapped the baby in a blanket, took the small body out into the bush, and left it. A few days later, a dog appeared, eating the baby's body. The grandmother told the police that since the baby had died while she was gone, Scovia must have killed her son. Although no other facts suggest that Scovia lied, a simple accusation was enough to arrest her and charge her with murder.

Another case involved a fourteen-year-old orphan from the Congo who moved to Uganda. A police officer found him in the streets and allowed the boy to stay with him at the police barracks because they were both members of the Lango tribe. Others at the barracks harassed him because of his distinctive ethnic features. Hopelessly discouraged with life, he stole a gun from the storage area to kill himself. Before he went through with the plan, police arrested him for possession of a firearm.

As we worked, we found simple acts—the things we discovered right in front of us—left the biggest impressions. A boy named Sunday was accused of rape and arrested without notice to his family. Sunday and his father had not seen each other in two years. The father did not have twenty-five dollars to make the round trip. We called him and paid for him to come for an interview. He traveled for hours on the back of a motorbike. After the interview, we took him out to the remand home with us, and he sat with his son under a tree. Twenty-five dollars reunited a family. If we had not been there—if we had not shown up and made this tiny gift—the family could still have been waiting.

After finishing the interviews, we promised to return to the remand home for a game of soccer that afternoon. The boys eagerly awaited the game. The warden permitted them out of the building to join us. For the next hour we were simply present with the kids. We did nothing to help their cases; we played with them as equals. We were friends. Everyone felt free.

For part of the game, I didn't play. I sat in the grass taking photos and watching everyone. It reminded me of the scene in *The Shawshank Redemption* where Andy Dufresne offers to help one of the guards with a tax dilemma. At first Andy's comment almost costs him his life, but the genuine offer to help eventually gains Andy and his coworkers three beers each. As all the prisoners relax on the roof, enjoying their drinks, Andy sits to the side with a smile on his face. Red, the character played by Morgan Freeman, delivers the iconic line about Andy: "We sat with the sun on our shoulders, feeling like free men. . . . Me, I think he did it just to feel normal again, if only for a short while."

In that moment of presence on the soccer field, there were no prisoners. We were all free. The kids felt normal again, if only for a short while.

That evening we began to work and worked feverishly through the night. Coffee flowed freely as we furiously constructed case briefs on each child. The printer we had carried with us from the States worked overtime spitting out drafts. Our hotel became our war room as we commandeered the restaurant for the night and into the morning.

With paper and legal pads strewn everywhere, our team spread out, typing, editing, and printing until about 3 a.m., when the stapler bound its final case summary—one for the court file, one for the legal aid lawyer appearing on behalf of the children, one for the High Court justice, and one for us.

We promised the children we would make one last visit to the remand home before leaving. The kids waited for us, gathering together for a good-bye. Ray showed them the briefs prepared on their behalf, Jim presented them with school supplies for self-study in the remand home, and David called them up—one by one—to present copies of photos of each of them with us.

As we prepared to leave, the kids sang us a song they all knew. The first verse was in Swahili, and then the next two verses were in English: "Let the Spirit of the Lord come down.

. . . Let the angels of the Lord come down." As we reflected on our week, this song summarized much of it. On one hand, we felt, as humbly as can be said, that the Lord had sent us as his angels to "go and do" for these kids. On the other hand, we felt that the kids were sent to show us things we needed to change about ourselves.

When we at long last drove off down the red dirt road from the remand home and onto the highway, we remained gripped in somber silence for the first hour. With all the windows rolled down, the sweet African air aided reflection.

On our last night before leaving Uganda, I went to David's hotel room. I brought a video camera and told him we would record the candid reflections still fresh in our minds. He said he wasn't prepared, but all the better; I wanted raw, unprocessed impressions.

For the first ten minutes David started recounting our trip as if reading the itinerary. Then he paused, as if he were tearing up his notes.

"It hit me that I had met God," David shared. "I met God in Masindi, Uganda. In some ways for the first time in my life. I've always known about God, and my whole life I have believed in God and tried to live a life of trust and faith. But I realized I'd never really known God. Sitting in the shade of that tree, talking to those kids, I was really looking need in the face eye to eye, shaking its hand, hearing its story, and trying to help. The disciples asked Jesus, 'When did we see you thirsty and give you drink and see you hungry and give you food? We don't remember doing that.' Jesus said, 'When you did it for the least of these.' These were the least of these. I realized about halfway through this trip that the face of those kids was the face of God. He's there. So for me, this trip was really me meeting God."

David had encountered God by going and doing in a way

he had not been able to before. Like David, you can't walk away from an encounter with the true and living God without being changed.

I sat Jim down in front of the camera, too, because I knew he was thinking. Jim is drawn to pain—someone who truly wants to share the yoke of a burden, as he does for his students. Jim found himself drawn to Henry in one of those deep, mysterious bonds as if you've been stuck together with God's glue.

Jim recalled a moment when Henry asked for Jim's phone number. Henry kept a secret cell phone hidden among his few personal items in the remand home—the warden knew, but he overlooked it because it allowed him to leave the premises and check in periodically by calling Henry. So when Henry asked for his phone number, Jim found himself at the crossroads of whether this relationship would continue beyond this weekend in Uganda. Jim paused and then gave Henry his office phone number.

Throughout the trip Ray the Litigator had spoken often of his own kids and listened to the Goo Goo Dolls' song "Better Days" on repeat: " . . . and the one poor child who saved this world, and there's ten million more who probably could, if we all just stopped and said a prayer for them."

Jesus had divine resources at his disposal, yet he took on very humble origins when he came to earth. The song reminds me of the importance of each and every child, that they all have incredible potential to offer the world. It's easy to get lost in the sheer size of the problem—the millions of orphaned children in Uganda. We can't lose sight of those who end up right in front of us, and when we see them, we must do as much as we can.

Before Ray left Uganda, he seriously considered returning the following week to attend the hearings. Work and family responsibilities made it impossible, although I had a feeling he would be back—I could see his wheels turning all week about the possibilities. Two months after our initial trip I received an e-mail from Ray recommending that someone from our team return to be present at one of the last, and most important, hearings. Ray told us not to hold back from going. We shouldn't be stopped by fear, uncertainty, and not knowing what else to do. He encouraged everyone to have faith in God, as he guides our actions for the good of mankind. This was a different, unbridled Ray from the one who almost didn't make the trip. "Go and do" had sparked something in him.

In the coming months we followed the cases of the kids we had worked with. Our briefs were able to resolve Henry's first murder case and he and his brother were acquitted and released. But Henry still had a second case against him—the second murder accusation. In that case, despite what we believed to be strong evidence to the contrary, the judge found Henry guilty. Another court appearance was arranged for sentencing—an appearance that would determine whether Henry walked out on probation or did two to three more years in jail.

Two days after hearing the first verdict, Jim bought a ticket and boarded a plane bound for Uganda, again uncertain of exactly what he would do. He simply knew he must go. He arrived in Uganda if only to be present with Henry for a few days. Jim also began writing a sentence mitigation brief to convince the judge that Henry should be released on bail and allowed to attend the Restore Academy in northern Uganda. The hope was that at Restore, Henry and his brother Joseph would receive one of the best educations in Uganda. Jim filed the briefs before leaving and began the long process of appealing Henry's conviction. Jim, who said that he would never consider taking his wife to Uganda—and made me skeptical that he would ever return—recently pulled his kids out of school, moved the whole family to Uganda, and embarked on an adventure to see what they can all accomplish together as a "go and do" family.

For me, I found joy in watching my colleagues come alive as they embarked on the "go and do" journey. From their "deer in the headlights" expressions upon arrival to the solemn drive back after finishing our work in the remand home, their week in Uganda had burned a desire to stay with the kids. Each member of our team came alive. Everyone experienced God in a new way. Watching my teammates felt like watching myself on my first trip to Thailand. I understood their passion, their grief, and their joy.

Of course, you don't have to be a professor, a litigator, or an environmentalist to go and do. Jim, Ray, David, and I are nothing extraordinary. We aren't celebrities, world leaders, or representatives of a major humanitarian organization. We are all ordinary people, and we bring whatever we can to the table.

Due to our presence and the case briefs we wrote, the judge released nineteen of the children. As the judge handed down each decision, we celebrated the victory of justice.

With the help of Restore International, the Lango boy on the verge of suicide was placed in a foster home located in a village of Lango people. Today he is happily making a new life there.

Joseph and Henry love school and quickly found themselves at the top of their class. Jim sponsors Henry's education and started writing his own book about his relationship with Henry, a look into Henry's life and the bond that God can form between two very different people. Jim continues to work diligently on Henry's appeal, which may take years to even bring to trial. Once his case is resolved and he is finished with school, we hope that Henry might attend Pepperdine. Jim and Henry continue to talk on the phone every Thursday morning, and until returning with his family, Jim's heart ached daily to be back in Uganda.

David's mind dwells on Uganda every day. Months after returning, we found out that David undertook complicated legwork from the United States to contact the internally displaced persons camp we visited. With the help of a friend near the camp, they identified the girl in the pink dress, and David and his family now sponsor Brenda. She's doing very well in school. David and his entire family plan to go back to Uganda to visit her. Brenda is making David's family a go and do family.

The more I reflect on these days in Uganda, the more I'm reminded of the poem "No More Leaving," by Hafiz, the legendary Persian poet. Though not a Christian, Hafiz shares an intimate encounter relevant to understanding the nature of our Christian God:

At
Some point
Your relationship
With God
Will
Become like this:
Next time you meet Him in the forest
Or on a crowded city street
There won't be anymore
"Leaving."
That is,
God will climb into
Your pocket.
You will simply just take
Yourself
Along![25]

God climbed into each of our pockets in Uganda. We were regular people. We looked at what we had—our professions—and chose to preach the gospel through action. It wasn't so much about our skill sets as it was about doing *something*—whatever we found right in front of us. Getting to the "go" part was challenging for each of us, but we took a leap of faith. And we got to the "do" part of faith by being present and dreaming the bold idea that justice could be done in the most challenging of circumstances. We were ambassadors for God, and we did our best to show his love to a prison full of kids who may only have seen it for the first time.

We all changed ourselves. And in the end, we changed the world for twenty-two children.

Epilogue

WHEN I DARED MYSELF to take a summer and dedicate it to "go and do," little did I know that I was entering God's great exchange program and mutual rescue plan.

Along the way I saw why more people fail to discover this same joy in their lives. The obstacles to "go and do" may at times seem insurmountable. The labyrinth of life becomes daunting, and the rigors of discipline seem too much to reach the end of it. Many people get turned away from the center and find it easier to follow the path of least resistance. Those who get lost in the labyrinth wander into deserts far from joy and heroic purpose.

Like walking the prayer labyrinth I found in Thailand, when we face the challenges ahead of us, we must fix our eyes upon the center goal—meeting God. It's easy to lose sight of that on a path that twists and turns. At times it's easy to meander in directions opposite of where we want to go. And other times we realize that directions we thought were wrong were actually the best path to the center.

I know people who find themselves in deserts of joylessness— deserts they can wander through for years. If this is your experience and you feel a burning, maybe an unspoken desire to "go and do," then I dare you to try it.

Whether you feel as if you are in a desert or an oasis, what holds you back from figuring out what God could do with you? I dare you to treat your life as a grand experiment and see where exploring "go and do" might take you. I'll even give you a formula to follow.

Choose: Find a location or topic that makes you come alive. Is there a country, city, or neighborhood to which you've always found yourself drawn? Or is there a topic that you can't get off your mind? What keeps you up at night? What articles do you find yourself incessantly reading online? What fits your unique interests, skills, or profession? I find these to be tiny indicators of the paths God has laid out for us. It's these tiny glimpses of joy that begin orienting us toward him and the adventure he has planned.

Commit: Irrevocably plan to "go." Maybe it's one weekend, maybe it's a week, or maybe it's even a month or a year. Then, take the time off. Block it out on your calendar now and buy a nonrefundable plane ticket. Force yourself to "go." Most of all, commit to being open to adventure. Allow God to stir you wherever you land. Explore.

Show up: Reach out to organizations or people in the places you find yourself drawn to. Don't take no as a closed door. Sometimes you need to show up in person and do whatever you find right in front of you. Be strategic, but don't worry about every last detail. Don't let travel guides "own" you. Eventually you might find that you only need to plan where you will stay upon arrival and figure out the rest on the fly. Forget expectations and be flexible. Most important, prepare to simply be present. Leave the details to the great adventure that God has in store.

Invest: Don't "go and do" as a one-time thing, make it a lifetime commitment. Find one place you care about and return as often as you can—"adopt" a country, neighborhood, or cause. Sometimes the first trip hardly bears fruit—it takes continued presence to build trust and see results. Create friendships and give out your e-mail address and phone number. Be an ambassador for what you learn by telling the stories when you return. Maintain the friendships you build, then go back to show them you mean it. Make it a lifestyle.

The End of the Labyrinth

Not too long ago I found a new e-mail in my in-box from Brady the Revolutionary. Brady, the bearded college student in the army jacket who wanted to challenge his faith and change himself, wrote to me because he received an internship offer in India where he could spend a year investigating and combating bonded slavery.

In his e-mail Brady considered whether to take the leap of faith. Brady wrote that this represented "the biggest step of faith I think that I have ever made." I could tell he felt nervous—the good kind of nervous where you know that God is saying, "Okay, if you really trust me, then here you go. Here is what you wanted, but it's not going to be comfortable or easy." A few days later Brady wrote me again, telling me that he signed his name on the dotted line. He took the jump. He accepted the dare to "go and do." Brady wrote further about the sense of peace he felt and his excitement about what might be around the next turn in his labyrinth. He already saw glimpses of joy.

A few months later he sent another update, glowing about the experience. He wrote, "I still have moments where I can't believe how blessed I am to be here." It was hard for him to describe, and I understood that. At the end of the note, he concluded, "I do think it will be an odd experience to see what will happen when I go home and all those small ways I've changed will be exposed. My childhood home, family, and longtime friends will be like a beam of light exposing dust in the air that I wasn't aware of just moments before." Brady's personal revolution was starting to illuminate the areas that he may no longer see as spotless and clean. He would return different.

Brady had joined God's great exchange program.

Many of us need to be rescued from joyless deserts. With our great tension nearing the breaking point, we find ourselves wandering, lost, and wondering whether we are capable of anything more. But when God tugs at our hearts, it's time to make a change. It's time to look for those beacons of joy and glimpses of purpose that make us come alive. It's then that we arrive at the critical question, "what am I doing here?"

Thankfully, we have an exit. We all have the opportunity to participate in God's great exchange program—a vast mutual rescue where our need for heroic purpose meets another's need for survival. The exchange asks much of our faith. We are asked to live dangerously—to do things that require faith and risk. We are asked to dream bold dreams about God's vision and restoration for the world. And we are asked to explore, to be open to the adventure.

Yet at the same time this exchange requires very little of us—no special skills, no passwords, no secret handshakes. At the very least, the best thing we can offer is our presence. And for that, all we have to do is show up.

God's rescue plan may be written specifically for this point in history. The world is ours more than ever before. We can now look at the world in ways that previous generations could not have imagined. And the world is waiting. Like my experience in the auditorium and the students whom I work with every day have learned, we are called to tell great stories with our lives—the kinds of stories that Jesus wants us to tell. We are called to be there and to participate, even if in just some small way. We are called to matter.

And why do we matter? Because it's up to us. Each of us as individuals—and the movements that we build together through churches, families, and organizations—are more critical than ever before. There is no other plan, no backup. It's up to us to "go and do."

I promise that at the end of this "go and do" journey, you will find yourself to be a different person. You will find that you are meant to change the world by changing yourselves. You will find that you get to make a small corner of the world a better place. *You* get to write a part of the script in God's great story arc. There's nothing more fulfilling.

I dare you to join us.

Acknowledgments

I AM INDEBTED TO SEALY YATES. Without his continual encouragement and mentoring, *Go and Do* might never have come to fruition.

I am indebted to the wonderful Tyndale House Publishers team who, with excellence, carefully assisted me in crafting this message. Their diligent efforts are helping me to create much more than a book. I am especially thankful for Associate Publisher Lisa Jackson, who early on caught the vision for *Go and Do*.

I am indebted to the Pepperdine community for the opportunity to pursue this project. I am thankful for the encouragement of Bob Cochran, Tim Perrin, Jim Gash, and many others who created the space for *Go and Do* to be written and "go and do" to happen. I am thankful for Lauren Hartley's thoughtful feedback and willingness to "hold down the fort" when I needed to write. I am thankful for Judge Ken Starr, who encouraged me to write this book and fostered a "go and do" atmosphere. I am thankful for Herbert and Elinor Nootbaar, whose generosity embodies the "go and do" spirit and who will forever transform the lives of countless students.

I am indebted to my family. I am thankful for the unfailing encouragement and patience of my wife, Lisa. And I am thankful for the support of my parents, sister, and grandparents.

Notes

1. Gil Bailie, *Violence Unveiled* (New York: Crossroad Publishing, 1996), xv.
2. Margaret Mead, BrainyQuote.com, Xplore Inc, 2012, http://www
   .brainyquote.com/quotes/quotes/m/margaretme100502.html, accessed
   February 1, 2012.
3. Mark Labberton, *The Dangerous Act of Worship: Living God's Call to Justice*
   (Downers Grove, IL: InterVarsity Press, 2007), 63.
4. Gary A. Haugen, Commencement Address (commencement address,
   Pepperdine University School of Law, Malibu, CA, May 22, 2009).
5. Frederick Buechner, *Wishful Thinking: A Seeker's ABC* (New York: Harper
   Collins, 1993, revised and expanded edition).
6. TED: Ideas Worth Spreading, "Carne Ross: An Independent Diplomat,"
   filmed at Business Innovation Factory October 2009, posted September 2010,
   http://www.ted.com/talks/carne_ross_an_independent_diplomat.html.
7. Martin Luther King Jr., "Letter from Birmingham Jail," in the *Norton
   Anthology of African American Literature*, ed. Henry Louis Gates Jr. and Nellie
   Y. McKay (New York: W. W. Norton & Company, 1997), 1854–1866.
8. Paul Kelly, "Blair Sees the Real Power in Faith," *The Australian*, July 28, 2011.
9. George Neumayr, "Midland Ministers to the World," *The American Spectator*
   (December 2003/January 2004).
10. Ibid, XX.
11. Helen Keller, *The Open Door* (New York: Doubleday, 1957).
12. Gary Hamel, "Innovation's New Math," *Fortune*, July 9, 2001, accessed
    January 31, 2011. ARTICLE,http://money.cnn.com/magazines/fortune/
    fortune_archive/2001/07/09/306498/index.htm.
13. Peter Drucker, *The Essential Drucker: The Best of Sixty Years of Peter Drucker's
    Essential Writings on Management* (New York: Harper Collins, 2008), 283.

14. Shirley Chisholm. Thinkexist.com, 2011, http://thinkexist.com/quotes/ shirley_chisholm/, accessed February 9, 2012.
15. Henri J. M. Nouwen, *Gracias* (New York: Harper & Row, 1983) 147–148.
16. Anaïs Nin, *The Diary of Anaïs Nin, Volume Three: 1939–1944,* ed. Gunther Stuhlmann (New York: Mariner Books, 1971), 125.
17. David Platt, *Radical: Taking Back Your Faith from the American Dream* (Colorado Springs, CO: Multnomah Books, 2010).
18. Gary A. Haugen, *Just Courage: God's Great Expedition for the Restless Christian* (Downers Grove, IL: InterVarsity Press, 2008), 124.
19. Laird Hamilton, *Force of Nature: Mind, Body, Soul, and, of Course, Surfing* (Emmaus, PA: Rodale Books, 2010), 3.
20. Kevin Belmonte, *Hero for Humanity: A Biography of William Wilberforce* (Colorado Springs, CO: Navpress Publishing Group, 2002), 175.
21. Margaret Thatcher, interview by Brian Walden, *Weekend World,* London Weekend Television, January 6, 1980.
22. Belmont University, *Living a Better Story,* last modified February 1, 2012, http://www.belmont.edu/livingabetterstory/.
23. John Glenn, cited in "Glenn Space Adventure Strengthens My Faith," CNN.com, last modified February 2, 2012, http://articles.cnn.com/1998-11-01/tech/9811_01_shuttle.02_1_shuttle-astronauts-john-glenn-discovery-crew?_s=PM:TECH.
24. Frank White, *The Overview Effect: Space Exploration and Human Evolution* (Reston, VA: American Institute of Aeronautics and Astronautics, Inc., 1998), 11, 12.
25. Hafiz, *The Gift,* trans. Daniel Ladinsky (New York: Penguin Compass, 1999), 258.